The Buddha Book

Spiritual means the mind, and spiritual people are

those who seek its nature. Through this they come

to understand the effects of their behavior, the

actions of their body, speech, and mind. Morality is

the wisdom that understands the nature of the mind.

When you know the nature of your own mind, depression

is spontaneously dispelled. Whatever pain, pleasure, or

other feeling you experience, it is all an expression of your

mind. When you discover that true satisfaction comes only

from the mind, you realize you can extend this experience

without limit, and then it is possible to discover everlasting

happiness … so it is actually very simple.

LAMA YESHE

LILLIAN TOO

Photography by Geoff Dann

The Buddha Book

Buddhas, blessings, prayers, and rituals to grant you love, wisdom, and healing

Inspired by the teachings of Lama Kyabje Zopa Rinpoche

GRAMERCY BOOKS
NEW YORK

I dedicate whatever merit arises from this book to the long life of most
precious guru, Lama Kyabje Zopa Rinpoche, to whom I prostrate, make
offerings and go for refuge. May all his holy wishes be fulfilled immediately. May His Dharma inspired projects in India, Mongolia, Australia,
United States, Asia and Europe to benefit sentient beings actualize and
meet with success, including the building of the world's largest Buddha
statue of Maitreya Buddha in India.

This 2005 edition is published by Gramercy Books,
an imprint of Random House Value Publishing,
a division of Random House, Inc., New York,
by arrangement with HarperCollins*Publishers*, London.

Gramercy is a registered trademark and the colophon
is a trademark of Random House, Inc.

Random House
New York • Toronto • London • Sydney • Auckland
www.randomhouse.com

Printed and bound in Hong Kong by Toppan

A catalog record for this title is available
from the Library of Congress.

ISBN 0-517-22514-X

10 9 8 7 6 5 4 3 2 1

one

two

three

four

five

six

seven

eight

nine

Contents

On Life

Life is ...
like a flickering flame:
a phenomenon that
cannot last long.
Like an illusion:
appearing real
but not there—
being empty.

Phenomena are
like dewdrops
or water bubbles
that can perish any time.

Being transitory in nature
like a dream
they appear real
from their own side,
yet they are empty from
their own side.

Like a dream—
exactly like that.
Total hallucination
Like lightning,
transitory in nature.
When there is lightning
a flash of light appears
and then it is gone.

Same:
When death comes
all appearance of this life
go,
like friends who were here
then pass away
and are gone.

Buddha said:
If we cling, if we grasp
there is suffering.
Things cannot last;
they are impermanent by
nature.
Holding the view of
permanence
only leads to suffering.
It creates the cause to
reincarnate in samsara
again.

Attachment ties us to
samsara ... again.

From Lama Kyabje Zopa Rinpoche's teaching on Impermanence, given at Losang Drakpa Buddhist Meditation Center, Kuala Lumpur, Malaysia, on February 2 2002.

Meeting a Living Buddha
My Personal Journey into Bliss

My journey began in the holy city of Bodhgaya, in India. Several years ago, in February 1997, I had the great good fortune to meet one of the most amazing beings of our time, someone whom I unexpectedly recognized. This strange sensation of déjà vu hit me at the moment when his palms pressed against the sides of my head as I bowed instinctively and presented him with the symbolic offering of a silk scarf. This gesture and ritual are very much a part of the Tibetan Buddhist tradition each time one meets a recognized high lama (guru).

The sensation of "remembering" happened at some uncanny, experiential level. One moment I was curiously anticipating meeting a holy man, and the next this almost blissful sense of recognition came over me. I felt drawn to him as if he were someone I had known and loved for a very long time. The feeling was momentary – like a television channel flickering for an instant – before switching back to the mundane world where I was being introduced to Lama Kyabje Zopa Rinpoche.

In this life, that was our first meeting. He was smiling in no special way; he did not pick me out for special attention. I was one in a long line of people waiting to offer a *kata*, the traditional silk scarf. But as Rinpoche's disciples and followers knelt and prostrated all around me in reverence to him, I recall thinking, "What took him so long to find me?"

REMEMBERING A PAST LIFE

Since then I have embraced Lama Kyabje Zopa Rinpoche as my spiritual guide and teacher. It was a meeting I should have anticipated, but when you really do not know anything about lamas and past lives, this is not something you could realize.

There had been many signs, but I was blind to them. Most telling had been my dreams, of which the most significant was one of two white tigers, which I later discovered were in fact snow lions. These heralded the appearance of the guru into my life, although I was unaware of this. Then there had been the continuous mental images that came to me –

images of some distant time, up in the Himalayan mountain range and on the stone-cold floor of a monastery. Later I would understand them to be flashes of memory, but when they first came into my consciousness they meant nothing to me. It was only when I saw pictures and actually went to the Solu Khumbu region in the Himalayas that I recognized the place. Those revelations blew my mind, but even then I bent over backward not to "reach" out. I kept dismissing the coincidences as fancy imagination on my part – until I met Rinpoche, and felt the momentous impact of that up-close moment.

For a year after that personally historic meeting, I flew around the world chasing Buddhas – I went from India to Taiwan to the United States, and eventually to Kathmandu and the Himalayas, to the high mountains of the Solu Khumbu region and a village called Lawudo. I am now convinced that in a past life I lived there with Rinpoche – at a time when he was the Lawudo Lama, a living Buddha who manifested as a meditator-teacher living in retreat in a cave in the high mountains. Few knew him for what he really was, until the time came for his passing on.

Only at his death did the Lawudo lama reveal the enlightened mind that had resided in his enlightened body. For twelve days and nights the signs appeared – rainbow clouds, blue skies, and the sounds of angels singing. After he had been cremated, nothing of the bones of his holy body remained among the ashes, save a precious jewel. This sparkling jewel was subsequently returned to his family ... and then the people of that region came to regard the Lawudo lama as an enlightened being. But there was much more to his kindness, for the stunning sequel of that magnificently divine passing was his reincarnation: the Lawudo lama came back.

He reincarnated into the body of the young Zopa Rinpoche, and from the moment he could talk he made known who he was, persistently pointing to the old Lawudo lama's cave and insisting that was his cave. Buddhists know that "divine happenings" always occur as if they are common-day occurrences, with little excitement and no fanfare. That is how it happened with the Lawudo lama's reappearance in the human realm – but, instead of coming back as a meditator living in a remote cave, this time he took the form of a humble monk. He easily passed all the tests that eventually led to his recognition and enthronement as the reincarnation of the Lawudo Lama. As a young tulku (reincarnate lama), Rinpoche spent some years in Tibet getting a monastic education, before being forced to flee to India when the Chinese invaded in 1959.

PAST LIVES AND NEW PERSPECTIVES

For years I had known that in a past life I lived in a cave overlooking a valley cultivated with bright-green plants (which I later discovered were potato plants), while in the distance there were high, snow-capped mountains. I knew that my significant past lives had to have been lived somewhere amid such peaks, for I have always loved mountains. For a long time I assumed that the picture in my mind was somewhere in China. It was only after I went to Lawudo that I realized that it was a vision of somewhere high up in the Himalayas.

Meeting Rinpoche made everything I had ever been and done take on a new perspective. I had retired from corporate life in the early 1990s, after reaching some exalted heights. No one believed I could make myself get off the roller-coaster life I had carved out in the rich and glamorous world of business.

I told skeptical friends I had "other mountains to climb." I had no idea what lay ahead, but had retired to become a full-time mother. It seemed absurd, after praying so hard and taking a decade to produce a child, to turn away from the joys of mothering Jennifer in favor of chasing the corporate dream. So I cashed in my investments, made myself redundant, packed my bags, said goodbye to Hong Kong, and went home to Malaysia. I devoted the next few years exclusively to Jennifer – it was a special time for us both and one we will never forget. In those few years Jennifer blossomed, and between us was born a mother-daughter love that today transcends our hearts and minds. But we are two individuals. And while my life is entering its waning phase, hers is just beginning. As Jennifer's life takes on new colors and flavors, it makes me realize that I cannot live my life exclusively around hers. If I truly wish her to fly, I must let go.

I turned to writing, a first love that for twenty years I had put on hold. Feng shui seemed an obvious subject for me to make uniquely my own. Something must have impelled me to become an author of feng shui books, for my very first book on the subject – amateurish and self-published though it was – struck a chord with collective minds out there hungry for knowledge of the subject. Feng Shui became instantly successful. More importantly, it came to the attention of Lama Kyabje Zopa Rinpoche.

Like a single drop of water falling into a big pond, the ripples created by my first book had many repercussions – new-found fame and fortune, a new career, and a new way of life. Most importantly, the book became the instrument that led to a spiritual awakening that would leave me breathless, amazed, and hungry for more.

Through Feng Shui Rinpoche found me, and through Rinpoche I met the Buddhas. Through Rinpoche, I learned about past lives and reincarnations; about karma and the seeds of enlightenment; about the nature of the samsaric world and the ability to become liberated; about compassion, and the ultimate realization of wisdom that comes from understanding emptiness. Success, wealth, material gain – all the things that had meant so much to me beforehand now took on a new perspective. I saw them simply as part of this samsaric world, as temporary manifestations of past good karma, but I also knew that these material comforts and luxuries were impermanent. As with life itself, everything we have – our beautiful bodies, our wealth, and our health – is impermanent.

All of life is impermanent. All of life is in the nature of suffering. There is no permanent happiness. The only real and lasting happiness comes from the wisdom-mind that has realized compassion and emptiness – this is the true nature of reality.

This is the awakened mind, the enlightened mind, a state of mental consciousness that "neither exists nor does not exist." If you do not understand this last phrase, that is fine, for neither do I really, and neither do the millions who have studied the sutras (sacred texts). If we did understand, we would all have become Buddhas. But this is what we strive to comprehend – this is the realization that is the state of enlightenment. It is the sorrowless state, a state of no more learning; it is the state of awakening that we constantly strive to reach.

So in meeting my highest high lama, Buddha's teachings engaged my heart and my mind. I recall the scenery before me, and being seated behind the slightly bent back of my lama. I do not see his face. I only feel his presence and am overwhelmed with devotion. He is meditating and wears a light-colored robe. He bears no physical resemblance to my Rinpoche of this life. My conviction that they are one and the same comes from somewhere deep inside me. It is experiential, and I have no way of knowing if it is true. It is true for me only because I believe it. In this life, I know that my feeling for Rinpoche is something karmic, because I recognize him and I revere him. My devotion to Rinpoche as my guru from many past lives comes from somewhere within me. It requires no effort for me to revere him.

CONNECTING AGAIN IN THIS LIFE

After connecting again with Rinpoche in this life, wherever he happened to be I would try my hardest also to be – and the year I met him became unforgettable. My mind and head went into a tailspin that was painful and blissful at the same time. I think I had been blind for so long to the real nature of existence that the delusions of success, wealth, and glamor had made the ego and the self-cherishing mind excessively dominant. The cleansing process was painful and wrenching – it was all felt inside my head!

But Rinpoche was incredibly kind to me – in some past lives I must have done a few things right, for the good karma ripened magnificently. I met my Buddha and realized it. I recognized my teacher. I was ready for him when he materialized in my life.

So I did what he advised me to do. I chanted purifying mantras to cleanse away eons of negative karma. I changed my attitudes and made a real effort to show compassion for others. I watched my mind and made the effort to transform it. I studied the translated texts on mind transformation, attended precious teachings, took refuge and initiations that would bring me closer to the buddha-deities, and started practicing meditations and spiritual visualizations. It was all rather heady stuff, and many times my egoistic mind rebelled and I blew my top. But again and again I would come back to the path, to the Dharma (spiritual practice).

It did not take me long to see Rinpoche as an emanation of the great lineage of teachers who accept rebirth with the sole purpose of bringing the message of compassion and wisdom to many people. A special divine being, or holy bodhisattva, Rinpoche is one of the living buddhas who walk the face of the earth. Since beginningless time they have been among us, manifesting as humble monks or in other guises, and guiding those whose karma it is to meet and know them toward the ultimate bliss of enlightened existence. In meeting Lama Kyabje Zopa Rinpoche once again, I met my living emanation of Buddha, who was to show me amazing new pathways on which my mind could travel.

THE MULTITUDE OF BUDDHAS

Through Rinpoche, I met many other buddhas, who appeared in different forms and colors. There are white, red, green, yellow, and blue buddhas. There are buddhas with gentle, loving faces and benign expressions, and there are wrathful, fearsome buddhas. There are buddhas with the appearance of humans, and those that appear as frightful beings with animal heads. There are single- and multi-faced buddhas, just as there are buddhas with 1,000 arms and several eyes. There are buddhas who appear as a single entity, and buddhas who manifest with consorts. There are male and female buddhas.

Rinpoche has told me that there are 1,000 buddhas in this eon, and in the Diamond Cutter Sutra, Shakyamuni himself (the historical Buddha) refers to 840 billion billion buddhas … and he pleased them all before he attained enlightenment himself.

This revelation really blew my mind, because all my life I had thought of the Buddha as a single entity, as a "God presence." I had read the life story of the Buddha (see page 8). I had always described myself as a Buddhist when filling out forms, but it was meaningless because my idea of Buddhism was very limited. I suspect this is the case for many others – overseas Chinese like me, who come from a traditional Buddhist background, but whose knowledge of what this means is woefully limited. Getting to know the buddhas through Rinpoche opened my eyes to a glorious new world – one that conjured up rich, colorful images within the deepest recesses of my mind.

Once I was with Rinpoche in Singapore. It was the night of May 16, 1998 – I had requested to see him and had waited throughout the day. By the time Rinpoche's appointments were through, it was close to 2 a.m. I was very sleepy and, as we drove Rinpoche back to where he was staying, I could not prevent my disappointment from showing. I told him that I would wish him good night, as I was flying home early the next morning. That was when he surprised me. "Maybe you can take a shower," he smiled as he saw me stifling a yawn. I could not believe it! Rinpoche had gone from one meeting to the next – blessing a hospice, seeing a sick disciple, giving a teaching, sitting down to dinner with a group of Buddhists, and meeting hundreds of people, all eager to get blessings from him. Yet here he was at two o'clock in the morning still prepared to meet yet one more unimportant student – me!

This buddha is three hundred years old; I invited him into my home some fifteen years before meeting Lama Kyabje Zopa Rinpoche.

MEETING BUDDHA

That night was a major turning point for me, because Rinpoche gave me a picture of the guru "merit field" (see page 41) – a picture depicting all the gurus and all the buddhas in the sky – and he gave me a magnificent teaching on how to meditate on the merit field. He explained the different emanations of the buddhas and the essence of guru yoga practice (see page 38), the root of the spiritual pathway to enlightenment.

I think I really met Buddha that night. He came to me in the mind, body, and speech of my guru, and then I understood why devotion to your guru is so vital in the spiritual journey to enlightenment, to ultimate happiness, to the state of sorrowless bliss.

In the quiet of the night when the world was asleep, that May evening, Rinpoche closed his eyes and said simply, "You write." So I took out my pen and notebook and wrote as Rinpoche talked. His voice was low and he spoke slowly to make certain I did not miss a single word.

I discovered that night that my lama, my guru, is the manifestation of all the Buddhas' holy mind – what we call the Dharmakaya, which is the transcendental wisdom of non-dual bliss and voidness. The Dharmakaya is the unified primordial savior, which has no beginning and no end, the holy mind of the Buddhas. It pervades all existence, including my heart, my head, my hands, and so on. So my lama is in fact my absolute guru, and is bound by infinite compassion toward me and all other sentient beings. He manifests and benefits me and all sentient beings, bringing us from happiness to happiness; to liberation from samsara (cyclic existence); and especially to the highest enlightenment.

The explanation of the emanation of the guru as embodying the Buddha's holy mind is simple. Because our minds are impure, blinded by karmic obstacles, we are prevented from seeing the divine presence of the buddhas. So numberless buddhas can appear in front of us, and because of the obscured nature of our minds we do not have the ability to see them. So buddhas, in their great compassion, emanate as ordinary beings.

The pure but ordinary form that we can "see" is the conventional guru, and that the guru's holy mind is the absolute guru. So those of us who are fortunate enough to meet perfectly qualified lamas have, in effect, met "buddhas" in their ordinary aspect. This is the aspect that can guide us from the lower realms to the human realms, from samsara to enlightenment.

It is understanding this that makes us realize that even the ordinary aspect of the Buddha is extremely precious. And all the numberless buddhas – Shakyamuni, Tara, Maitreya,

Vajrasattva, Amitabha, and so on – all the buddhas of this eon can guide us, interact with us, through the ordinary aspect of the guru. This is why when we meet a lama who can lead us on the journey to enlightenment he becomes the most precious and most kind being – the most important being – in our life.

Because without him we are lost in samsara – guideless, moving from one rebirth to the next, unceasingly creating causes for rebirth in the lower realms and ignorant of the way to attain liberation and ultimately reach the sorrowless state of enlightenment. It is the lama, or guru, who embodies all the buddhas, and realizing this becomes the foundation of the spiritual journey to bliss.

Buddhas are best thought of as a visualized presence. And since we are unable to "see" real buddhas, images of them also become extremely precious, because they can help us imagine their presence. Thus pictures, thangka paintings on cloth, statues (also known as rupas), and all forms of Buddhist art are revered as precious holy objects, because they actually help us "see" Buddha in our mind's eye.

Of course I have never seen or met any of the buddhas about whom Lama Kyabje Zopa Rinpoche has told me, except perhaps in dreams or when I am hallucinating. Yet meeting them, even through the dimension of visualization, has enriched my life in the most meaningful way. My home is filled with beautiful Buddhist art and it has become easy to visualize the light emanation of the buddhas, who for me have come to represent so many aspects of the spiritual path.

IT BEGAN IN BODHGAYA

Lama Kyabje Zopa Rinpoche took my heart as soon as I laid eyes upon him. In Bodhgaya – where the historical Buddha, Shakyamuni, attained the perfect state of enlightenment – I began my tentative steps on the path to enlightenment.

Rinpoche had communicated his holy wish for me to come to Bodhgaya to advise on the feng shui of a giant Maitreya Buddha statue, whose construction was being planned. I was not confident that I could single-handedly accept such a responsibility, but a request from such a high lama could not be ignored. So I flew to India, even though I had never previously met or heard of Lama Kyabje Zopa Rinpoche. His approach to me came in a letter faxed from America, and my response was a purely instinctive one.

It did not take me long to realize my great good fortune in having met Rinpoche under such wonderful circumstances. Shortly after the Bodhgaya meeting, Rinpoche came to Malaysia to give a series of teachings and to conduct a one-week spiritual retreat in the mountains just outside Kuala Lumpur. In those few days I took the most intensive course imaginable in Mahayana Buddhism. It was a mind-blowing experience. I discovered what a perfectly qualified lama I had inadvertently met. I saw at first hand his awesome qualities of humility, compassion, and wisdom. There is an aura of purity around Rinpoche that words cannot describe.

I followed the Buddhist tradition and took "refuge" with Rinpoche. This is the process of officially becoming his student and taking him as my lama, thereby entering into a guru-disciple relationship. He let me participate in the Great Chenrezig initiation, a Buddhist ritual that opened further new worlds to me. In the months and years that have followed, Rinpoche has introduced me to a stunning pantheon of buddhas – each personifying some aspect or dimension of the enlightened mind.

In time I would learn the secret teachings of Buddha, engage in the practice of sadhanas (meditative visualizations), make offerings, prostrations, and circumambulations, recite the magical mantras, learn the visualizations, and, most importantly of all, learn the bodhisattva way of life, which would put me on the quick path to enlightenment. I was to come to understand the bodhisattva vows and the mind-training that would make my bodhichitta heart arise. All of these terms seemed strange then, but over time I was to develop an easy familiarity with them ... just as you will, as you meet the buddhas in this book.

If you have read this far, let me take you with me on my journey of bliss into the boundless. Let me introduce you to some of the buddhas of this fortunate age – the tathagatas, the fully enlightened ones, the foe-destroyers, the conquerors – all in their compassionate aspect. Look closely at the images so that you, too, may attune your mind to meeting the buddhas at an inner level, taking them into your heart and mind as you seek the awakening of ultimate happiness.

Do not engage in any harmful actions;

Perform only those that are good

Subdue your own mind –

This is the teaching of the Buddha

GURU SHAKYAMUNI BUDDHA

Meeting the Founder~ Buddha, Shakyamuni

Shakyamuni Buddha's meditation and visualization

This wonderful, fifteen-minute meditation can be practiced each morning. Sitting cross-legged, ideally in the lotus position, the back is held straight. The mind is calmed and thoughts turn to contemplation. The purpose of the meditation is considered: to embark on the spiritual path that will lead to awakening wisdom. The breath is rhythmic and steady.

Now a beautiful, bright-blue sky is visualized, stretching into the beyond just at the edge of consciousness. A sense of the cosmos pervades the mind, body, and spirit.

An awareness is brought to the level of the forehead; a large golden throne, beautifully adorned with all kinds of precious gemstones and jewels, is visualized. At each corner is a pair of snow lions, signifying the fearlessness of the buddhas. On top of the throne is a fully opened lotus, signifying the Buddha's holy mind. On the lotus are a sun disk and a moon disk. The sun signifies wisdom and the moon, method. Together they represent the unification of no more learning (the ultimate achievement: buddhahood). Seated upon them is the historical buddha Shakyamuni, who signifies the attainment of this unification. The lotus, sun, and moon also symbolize the principal aspects of the path to enlightenment.

As this image is held in the mind, one thinks how Shakyamuni Buddha, who took rebirth in the human realm, manifested the attainment of perfect realization – enlightenment – and then left the world the legacy of his teachings. As the ultimate teacher, the guru, he is therefore inseparable from one's own "root guru" (see page 26).

Buddha's golden body and aura radiate infinite compassion. He wears the saffron robes of a monk. His face is beautiful and his eyes see all beings. His gaze is peaceful, and his mind is free of all critical thoughts. He fully accepts everyone.

Buddhist art is an immensely valuable aid to visualization. In the thangka paintings of the Tibetan tradition, which are painted on cloth, the artist incorporates colorful symbolic imagery. Shakyamuni's right hand touches the earth, signifying control over the maras* of desire and attachment. His left hand holds a bowl of nectar, symbolizing the conquest of the cycle of samsara. His body is in the vajra posture, signifying that he has destroyed death and his own four maras. The light beams that surround Shakyamuni show that he is working compassionately for all beings.

*enemies of the mind.

BUDDHA'S HOLY MANTRA

TAYATA OM MUNE, MUNE, MAHA MUNEYE SOHA

A mala (a rosary repeated 108 times) of Buddha's holy mantra is recited, while holding a mental image of the glorious Shakyamuni Buddha. Looking at a picture or a thangka painting (see page 3) can help with this. As the mantra is recited, the person meditating visualizes golden-yellow light rays emanating from the Buddha's body and entering their own body through the crown of the head. It brings down a shower of blessings.

Closing the eyes can intensify the visualization experience. The mantra symbolizes the concentrated essence of the Buddha's wisdom and compassion. Reciting the mantra and simultaneously doing the visualization represents a powerful purifying practice, which brings a mountain of merit. Mantras may be chanted aloud (but not too loud) or recited in the mind – reciting them aloud is better, as it engages the speech as well as the mind.

Reciting the mantra 108 times is traditional, but it can be recited as many times as is desired. This practice results in a very blissful, calm state, which causes a beautiful spiritual awakening. When the practice is finished, the person sits quietly, and feels themselves receiving Buddha's blessings. Those who have a guru imagine that he is inseparable from the Buddha. Those who do not yet have a guru dedicate their mantra and visualization to meeting a perfectly qualified teacher who will help, guide, and empower their practices.

It is vital to make a dedication at the end in order to lock in the merit of the meditation. If this is omitted, then the merit created is wasted. The moment a person loses his temper, for instance, all the merit that has been accumulated evaporates.

The teachings of Shakyamuni Buddha are the basis of Buddhism. This hand mudra is known as Dharmachakra, or the mudra of teaching.

The path to enlightenment

In this present age, when we are living through the excellent eon of the 1,000 buddhas, the path to total enlightenment is founded on the teachings of Shakyamuni, the historical Buddha and the fourth of the 1,000 buddhas who will appear in our world. Maitreya Buddha, the Buddha of the future, will be the fifth Buddha (see Chapter 9).

A buddha is a fully enlightened divine being who has awakened from the sleep of ignorance, so that he has expanded all his awareness and all his senses. His body, speech, and mind are completely pure. His wisdom-mind is perfect wisdom, and his compassion is limitless compassion. The enlightened state of a buddha transcends all suffering and death. His is the omniscient mind that knows all things.

A buddha is not a Creator God. Evil and suffering, goodness and happiness are all part of the order of things produced by karma (see pages 21, 60) since beginningless time. The root of suffering lies in ignorance, which leads to misconceptions about the true nature of existence. Ignorance views the self as absolute, as separated from others. Ignorance leads to attachment, which in turn leads to desire and greed. Ignorance also leads to cravings that result in jealousy and anger. These in turn lead to stealing, killing, war, and many other negative events that create suffering. Suffering leads to bad karma, which in turn leads to the endless cycle of birth, death, and rebirth – referred to as samsara (see pages 21, 62–63).

Buddha's teaching is to eliminate ignorance. While Buddha cannot change our karma, he can teach us how to purify it, thereby reducing its severity. Buddha also teaches us the wisdom that totally understands the true nature of reality – the wisdom of "dependent arising," of knowing that the existence of self is dependent on and related to others. Understanding the nature of self leads to love and compassion. So the state of buddhahood is described as the greatest good, the highest happiness, the most supreme compassion, the most powerful love – it is a state of superlative being to which every living being can aspire.

A standing Shakyamuni Buddha with prayer wheel at Boudhanath stupa, Kathmandu, Nepal. Buddhas and Bodhisattvas manifest as prayer wheels to purify negative karma on the path to enlightenment.

The story of Shaykamuni Buddha

More than 2,500 years ago, in the sixth century BC, in what is now southern Nepal, a prince and heir is born to the Shakya clan. He is called Siddhartha and has the family name Gautama. His father is the ruler of the state, King Shudodhana. His mother, Maya, dies soon after Siddhartha's birth and it is his aunt, Mahaprajapati, who brings up the boy under the watchful eye of the king.

A glorious future is predicted for the young prince. He will grow up to be a great and holy teacher or a powerful monarch, the astrologer Asita tells the king. But the king wants his son to succeed him and instinctively fears this might not be. He knows that the young prince's sensitive nature could turn him into a philosopher, thereby causing him to surrender his birthright. So the king takes extreme measures to screen his son from the harsh realities of the outside world, and Siddhartha grows up in pleasurable isolation within the palace walls, carefully protected from the real world. Eventually he marries the beautiful princess Yasodhara.

Alas for the king, his carefully laid plans crumble when, at the age of twenty-nine, Siddhartha discovers the reality of city life beyond the palace gates. He encounters in quick succession the manifestations of life's suffering and impermanence – sickness, old age, and death – aspects of life that had been carefully shielded from him. The young prince realizes that all his worldly pleasures, his strong body, and even his life cannot protect him from these creeping forces. He has to confront the inevitability of suffering caused by the impermanence of life and of all things. Siddhartha realizes that his luxurious existence will one day cease and crumble away. These revelations bring despair and his thoughts weigh heavily on his mind. An intense compassion wells up within him.

One day, Siddhartha encounters a homeless wanderer dressed in monk's robes, whose demeanor belies his appearance, for the man carries himself like a nobleman. Siddhartha is inspired by the wandering mendicant's search for the true nature of life and identifies with the goal of finding the truth. He makes up his mind to quit the palace to search for answers that can overcome the suffering nature of existence.

The birth of his son, Rahula, strengthens his resolve. Compassion again wells up within him as he realizes that one day his son, too, will have to confront the inevitability of illness, old age, and death. On the night of a full moon, Siddhartha steals out of the palace and rides into the night on his white horse, Kanthaka, while deities support its hooves to muffle the sound. Turning his back on his family and his princely life, he hopes one day to return with answers.

The prince's determination leads him to study with two famous spiritual teachers, Alara Kalama and Udraka Ramaputra. From them, he acquires techniques of deep meditative absorption, which enable him to attain heightened states of consciousness that bring feelings of great bliss. But these states do not provide the answers Siddhartha is seeking. Death still remains the final reality.

Next he tries the path of intense asceticism. Looking at his body, he surmises that this that is the cause of suffering, so perhaps answers may be found in overcoming its physical demands. Denying the body food and sustenance will perhaps enable it to reach a state whereby he can escape the suffering of illness and old age. So Siddhartha fasts until he is skin and bone. He practices breath control until he nearly keels over. In his determination to discover a realm beyond old age and death, he subjects his body to intense agony and austerity. This discipline transforms his will into steel.

Five other ascetics practice alongside him, and for six years Siddhartha lives in this state of self-denial. But the answers and wisdom that he seek continue to elude him. He begins to realize that denying the body may not be the solution. His health suffers and this makes his mind weak; it is getting clouded and he is making no progress. It seems important to try another way, perhaps a middle road. So Siddhartha accepts some milk rice from Sujata, the wife of a local farmer. This disgusts his fellow practitioners, who believe that his will has weakened, so they abandon Siddhartha and leave for the Deer Park at Sarnath.

Alone, Siddhartha contemplates the new-found strength of his body. Making a cushion from patches of cut grass, he sits in the shade of what will later be identified as the bodhi tree. He resolves to meditate until he finds the path that will lead him to some answers and so bring a permanent end to all suffering.

His mind now takes on an intense clarity, lighting up vast beacons of memory from deep within – he remembers all his past lives and notes the cyclical patterns of birth, death, rebirth, and death, moving relentlessly in a never-ending rhythm. He sees all the beings of the world going through the same cycle. He contemplates how those who have been generous, kind, and loving experience rebirth in happy circumstances, while those who act with hatred, jealousy, anger, and greed inevitably fall into the suffering realms. It is all very clear. Birth and death seem wrapped around the sensations of craving, attachment, and the desire for living. It seems as if the cycle goes on forever.

It is the night of the full moon when Siddhartha begins, and as he sits in contemplative meditation he is continually "attacked" by maras – disturbing forces of delusion that try every way to break his concentration. First come temptations that are placed in his path – wealth and pleasure; then come threats that use fear as an agent of distraction; when this fails, the final weapon is the planting of seeds of doubt in his mind.

But the prince sits unmoved and undisturbed. Then, without breaking his concentration, he extends his right hand and touches the earth with his middle finger. Instantly the earth goddess appears to testify that the meditating prince has in past lives practiced the Six Perfections of generosity, morality, patience, enthusiastic perseverance, concentration, and wisdom. In touching the earth, the Mara forces are defeated and Siddhartha attains a total cessation of all suffering of body and mind, all ignorance and self-centeredness. Time and space vanish, and all ties melt away. In their place there is only total clarity, compassion, and wisdom consciousness, a state that is formless, with no beginning and no end – the state of all knowing; the state of no sorrow; the state of never-ending happiness and bliss!

The human personality of Siddhartha dissolves, and in its place emerges Shakyamuni, the historical Buddha, the supreme emanation, the enlightened One, the fully awakened One, the foe-destroyer. Buddha continues to sit, allowing the impact of the new wisdom to permeate his whole being. He is thirty-five years old when he attains enlightenment, and for seven weeks thereafter he remains in meditative repose, enjoying the state of matchless bliss.

Those who are not upset with suffering

and not attached to happiness

are free of obstacles to Dharma practice

are liberated from suffering and happiness

and will go to the city of the sorrowless state –

a blissful state of peace.

LAMA KYABJE ZOPA RINPOCHE

BUDDHA'S TWELVE DEEDS

The life story of Buddha is usually summarized as the twelve deeds of the Buddha, which are the twelve significant events of his life.

1.   Buddha descends from Tushita heaven to this world
2.   Buddha enters into his mother's womb
3.   Buddha's birth in Lumbini Garden, Nepal, to King Shuddhodana and Queen Maya
4.   Buddha becoming skilled in the arts and playing sports of youth
5.   Buddha's marriage to Princess Yasodhara, and his taking charge of the kingdom
6.   Buddha's renunciation at the age of twenty-nine
7.   Buddha's practicing austerities for six years
8.   Buddha sitting under the bodhi tree
9.   Buddha defeating the maras
10.   Buddha attaining enlightenment
11.   Buddha turning the wheel of Dharma
12.   Buddha attaining final parinirvana (complete nirvana, or liberation).

Buddhist art depicts each of these deeds in various ways, but it is the eleventh deed, the turning of the Dharma wheel (or the Buddhist teachings), that is most significant.

The life story of Buddha as shown in twelve separate scenes, reflecting the Twelve Deeds of Buddha.

shakyamuni's teachings

Shakyamuni's first teaching comes when he expounds the Four Noble Truths (see page 23) to his five ascetic companions in the Deer Park in Sarnath. Buddha explains these truths with immense clarity, but his five stubborn friends debate the profound implications of his words. Buddha is determined that they, too, should experience the matchless bliss of enlightenment, so his sermon goes on for a very long time.

One day, one of the ascetics suddenly realizes the same vision of truth that Buddha himself realized under the bodhi tree. Seeing this, Buddha is boundless with joy. It is an important breakthrough: if his disciple can achieve enlightenment, so all beings can obtain the realization that can set them free. Buddha's teachings will spread far and wide so that all beings blessed by them can attain the liberation that comes with enlightenment. This is the most profound impact of the story of Shakyamuni Buddha. He is the ultimate guru, who emanates in the earthly realm to pass on his teachings, without which ignorance will continue to prevail.

In all, Buddha leaves behind 84,000 teachings and these revered texts eventually become the foundation of the different traditions of Buddhism that spread across Asia in all directions. In Buddha's later years, it is Ananda who keeps accounts of his teachings and the events of his life. These are carefully preserved in the suttas (discourses) of the Pali canon and the sutras (scriptural texts) of the Kan Gyur.

Buddha passed away at the age of eighty in the village of Kushinagar, in what is today the Indian state of Uttar Pradesh. There he lay in the lion posture, on his right side, with his right hand supporting his head and his other hand placed lightly on his left thigh. His last words reminded his disciples that "all compounded things are by nature impermanent," and he advised them "in mindfulness" to strive on. It is recorded that on his deathbed, when asked by Ananda what should be done with his earthly remains, Buddha answered that, like those of a king, the remains of a tathagata (an exalted one) should be enshrined in a stupa (reliquary). To satisfy the demands of the kings and princes of the surrounding states, Buddha's relics were eventually divided into eight parts and placed in eight golden boxes (and so today there are eight types of stupa, each different in design). When the boxes were laid on the altar table, it is recorded that three rainbows arose from them. Below the relics were placed the five offerings of the senses: incense (sense of smell); food (sense of taste); flowers (sense of sight); music (sense of sound), and beautiful objects (sense of touch).

Monks performing holy puja
at Kopan Monastery, Nepal.

BUDDHA AND STUPAS

Ananda's records also reveal Buddha's advice on stupas. Buddha explains that when anyone sees a stupa and merely thinks, "This is the stupa of the Exalted One," the heart of that person will become calm and happy, and they would be reborn in the happy realms of the Pure Land (the western paradise of the Buddha Amitabha, see page 50). Even today, one of the most significant rituals that Buddhists of all traditions observe is circumambulation of the holy stupa. There are beautiful stupas in Borobodur in Indonesia and Myanmar (Burma). The two that I love to visit and highly recommend are Bouddhanath stupa in Kathmandu, Nepal, and the Mahabodhi stupa in Bodhgaya, India.

The legend of Boudhanath stupa reveals how it was built by a woman whose four sons dedicated the virtue to take rebirth as beings who were instrumental in bringing Buddhism to Tibet. It is said that one of the sons reincarnated as the great guru Padmasambhava (see page 130), who is regarded as the Buddha who brought Buddhism to Tibet, while another son reincarnated as the great king Songtsen Gampo (see page 134), who was responsible for spreading Buddhism across the country.

The Mahabodhi stupa is the fountainhead of Buddhism and the holiest pilgrimage place, for Buddha attained enlightenment in Bodhgaya. Circumambulating this stupa is incredibly purifying. As you walk clockwise around it, you can feel some of its energy embracing you and sending you into a very light place.

Happiness and sadness don't come from outside;

They come from one's own mind.

LAMA KYABJE ZOPA RINPOCHE

The stupa respresents Buddha's holy mind – Dharmakaya – and each part of the stupa shows the path to enlightenment. When seeing the Boudhanath stupa, Nepal, for the first time, close your eyes and make a fervent wish. It is said that anyone doing so will have their wish granted.

Basic Buddhism

Buddhism is both simple and profound. On a daily basis it advocates watching the mind so that all thoughts, actions, and words manifest a kind and compassionate attitude toward all others. It is the loving heart that places others above self. Herein lies the ultimate wisdom of existence. When you understand that the existence of all things, all beings, and all concepts is empty except in relation to other things, beings, and concepts, then you will be close to becoming awakened, so crossing into a state of permanent happiness.

When you succeed in eliminating ignorance and replacing it with real wisdom, suffering comes to an end, because in understanding the true nature of existence you are no longer bound by the illusions of samsara. You awaken and escape the endless cycle of birth, death, and rebirth.

When there is no end to samsara, then life and death are governed entirely by the laws of karma, so existence is a never-ending cycle of continuous rebirth in the Six Realms of Existence (see pages 61–63). The quality of your rebirth and the realm into which you are reborn are determined by your karmic score card. It is karma – the law of cause and effect – that gives life its moral code. The Buddha thus advised doing everything to create good karma, for this has the power to propel you into a rebirth in circumstances that are conducive to practicing Dharma, thereby having the chance to attain enlightenment. Practicing Dharma means showing generosity, having a good heart, purifying negative karma, and creating good karma. It also means embarking on the spiritual path that leads to enlightenment.

Fresco showing the Six Realms of Existence. Rebirth in the human realm is considered to be most conducive to the practice of Dharma – Buddha's teachings which show the path to enlightenment.

There are three types of karma: karma that you create and see its result in this life; karma that you create and see its result in your next life; and karma that you create and see its result after many lifetimes.

LAMA KYABJE ZOPA RINPOCHE

THE FOUR IMMEASURABLE THOUGHTS

When practicing Dharma, Four Immeasurable Thoughts should arise. These are:

1. Immeasurable equanimity – being free of the bias of liking some and disliking others, so remaining tranquil and unattached
2. Immeasurable compassion, wishing that all beings are freed from suffering
3. Immeasurable joy in the highest happiness and liberation of all beings
4. Immeasurable loving kindness, wishing for the happiness of all living beings.

Buddhism does not believe in a supernatural and omnipotent Creator God. Salvation does not come from the intervention of a divine entity. Instead, Buddha's teachings advocate the practice of compassion and loving kindness toward all living beings, combined with meditation practices to develop wisdom. It is the union of compassion and wisdom that leads to liberation and awakening.

Prayers to the buddhas are supplications to receive the wisdom to understand the true nature of reality – what are referred to as "realizations." Every living being possesses buddha-nature. It is by living a moral life, practicing compassion, and meditating on the steps that lead to the awakened mind that can be developed to high levels of concentration and wisdom, leading to enlightenment.

There are different schools of Buddhist practice, but all traditions focus on the Four Noble Truths and the Eightfold Path in order to achieve liberation from the cycle of rebirth. Mahayana Buddhism particularly emphasizes the attainment of enlightenment for the sake of all beings. Compassion and love for others represent the selfless, altruistic attitude that is paramount if you are to reach enlightenment.

THE FOUR NOBLE TRUTHS

1. All conditioned existence is suffering.
2. The causes of suffering arise from the afflictive emotions in our minds (attachment, anger, and ignorance).
3. There is a state in which all suffering has ceased.
4. The way to cease all suffering is to follow the Eightfold Path.

THE EIGHTFOLD PATH

1. Having the right understanding
2. Having the right aspiration
3. Having the right speech
4. Having the right conduct
5. Having the right livelihood
6. Making the right effort
7. Developing mindfulness
8. Developing concentration.

Today Buddhists of all traditions strive to keep Buddha's teachings uncorrupt and true to the original texts. Tibetan Buddhists are especially mindful that the words of Buddha can be traced back to their original source, since they have been carefully passed on from one realized master to another over hundreds and thousands of years. It is for this reason that teachings given by highly realized beings, such as the high lamas of Tibet or the master abbots of Buddhist temples in China, are considered so valuable. Like a bright lamp guiding us on a dark night, Buddha's words hold out the promise of permanent happiness and eternal bliss.

For many centuries, sacred texts containing the secret teachings of Buddha were carefully preserved in Tibet. The country and its beliefs were protected by high mountains, and the Buddhism of Tibet – the Mahayana and Vajrayana schools, which hold out the promise of enlightenment within a single lifetime – flourished. The invasion of Tibet by China in 1959 forced the Dalai Lama to flee the Land of Snows. Many high lamas followed him into exile, bringing with them precious teachings, valued lineages, and secret rituals and practices, which they are now sharing with the people of the world.

From the reincarnated high lamas – living buddhas and yogis – we can learn the meditations that will bring the highest purpose into our lives. We can learn to meditate on the Lam-Rim: the graduated path to enlightenment, the step-by-step way to attaining a peaceful and contented heart. But such a heart does not emerge suddenly. It comes from deep understanding, contentment, and genuine love, caused by overcoming greed, hostility, and ignorance. If you are to make spiritual commitment the center of your life, painstaking determination is required.

Transforming our rough, materialistic, and self-cherishing minds into the gentle and immeasurably kind heart of compassion is a long and winding road. For in truth we are embarking on the spiritual path to become saints and sages. We are, in effect, seeking the perfection of wisdom. Buddha knows that it is a hard journey. He has been through the process, so he sends emanations in earthly form to guide us, teach us, pick us up, and occasionally hold our hand.

Prayer flags hung in the wind adorn Buddhist monasteries. The flags send blessing energy in all ten directions, bringing purification and dissolving life's obstacles.

Seeking the Buddha's emanation: the guru

The Buddha sends the guru to us when we are ready. The guru is the emanation of Buddha's omniscient mind and, as we get closer to such emanations (be they humble monks, holy yogis, or recognized reincarnations of highly realized lamas of some past era), we become less obscured. We start to see the clear light that opens windows on the real nature of existence. We shed our ignorance and take on the wisdom that understands this true nature.

The guru is the most vital part of our spiritual journey, for without a guide we may get lost or lose sight of the essence of compassion and wisdom. The spiritual journey promises blissful enlightenment at the end, but it is not without its perils. At each step it is easy to fall into a lower-realm rebirth, unless you have the guiding hand of a truly compassionate teacher whose love and motivation are completely pure. There is no way of telling how long a time we each have; the only certain thing is that one day we will all die. Death can strike at any time, anywhere.

Much has been written about finding a guru, and the adage that "when you are ready, a guru will materialize" has proven true for many students and disciples with whom I have had the good fortune to converse. I discovered that each had his or her own extraordinary story of the moment when they made the connection and knew they had met their spiritual teacher. It is very special when you connect with a guru with whom you have complete affinity. When this happens, it becomes natural to develop a clear faith in your guru, and eventually to see his teachings and advice as that of the Buddha himself. It is this latter realization that creates a powerful reverence for him deep inside you and enables your guru to lead you along the path from one level to the next, until you reach enlightenment.

But seeking a guru (or what Tibetan Buddhists refer to as a lama) is not to be taken lightly. When you find one and take refuge with him, your whole life will change. Your value systems and attitude will undergo a major shift of emphasis. You will not be unaffected, whomever you follow, so it is vital to follow someone who will be exceptionally good for your spiritual progress. You must never compromise on the perfect quality of the one who will be guiding you and once the connection has been made, you must honor it with integrity.

Rinpoche explained to me that we often refer to the historical Buddha as Guru Shakyamuni Buddha. The word "guru" here describes Buddha's omniscient holy mind, which works for us, guiding us from suffering. We get close to his holy mind by taking "refuge" in perfectly qualified gurus.

THE TEN QUALITIES OF A HIGH LAMA

The Mahayana Sutra, *Maitreya's Abhisamayalamkara,* describes these ten qualities that a Mahayana teacher should possess.

1.   A mind subdued: through the higher training of morality
2.   A mind pacified: through the higher training of concentration
3.   A mind thoroughly pacified: through the higher training of wisdom
4.   More qualities than the disciple
5.   Perseverance: in working for others
6.   A wealth of scriptural knowledge: oral transmission and study
7.   A realization of emptiness according to the view of the Prasangika school
8.   Skill in teaching: according to the different levels of the disciples
9.   Love: for all beings in general and the disciples in particular
10.   No sense of weariness in teaching even the most difficult of disciples.

Westerners sometimes think monks and nuns are holy.

We're not holy; we're just trying.

LAMA YESHE

When I met my guru, Lama Kyabje Zopa Rinpoche, I was particularly taken by his abject humility, which is such an integral part of his whole being. And there is a special kind of joyousness in the way he speaks – laughter is never far from the corners of his eyes and mouth. I was quite bowled over, and I also felt rather humbled.

I had brought to our meeting all the negative baggage of a lifetime's worth of posturing and self-cherishing. There was a skepticism within me borne of the conviction that "I had seen it all …" – the kind of arrogance you find in anyone who has tasted success, power, and wealth. I really was rather full of myself! And I smoked like a chimney.

In Bodhgaya I was politely requested not to smoke in the presence of the high lama, and I recall slinking to the back of the building to light a cigarette every few hours. But here is the miracle. Soon after I returned from India I never touched another cigarette, and I have not smoked since. It was several months later that I realized that quitting smoking had something to do with meeting Lama Kyabje Zopa Rinpoche. Yet when I attempted to thank him, he did not even acknowledge that he had anything to do with it – that is the extent of his humility. Later there were many instances of Rinpoche's clairvoyance and his seemingly effortless ability to read my mind and know what I was about to say, before I gave voice to my thoughts. Yet each time I make reference to his "powerful magic," he will roar with laughter.

Since then I have come to realize that this is the way of high lamas. They are so incredibly humble that they never acknowledge their yogic powers. They create all kinds of phenomena, offer wise advice, demonstrate incredible clairvoyance, create cures, and heal many hearts by advising on spiritual practices, prayers, and mantras – yet they never take credit for the miraculous results that ensue. Lam Kyabje Zopa Rinpoche is always happy, no matter what time of the day or night and what problems have been placed before him. His mind is never troubled. And I have never seen him refuse to help anyone.

Lama Kyabje Zopa Rinpoche.

At first I developed a genuine respect for Rinpoche's awesome knowledge of the Dharma and his obvious goodness, but over time I came to see him as something much more than just a teacher. Each time he speaks to me, it is as if the Buddha is speaking directly to me:

The guru is the root of the path
He is the source of all my good.

Finding a lama and taking yourself to him in the correct way is the first step on the spiritual journey to enlightenment. It is like building a house: when the foundations are strong, the house is solid and lasts a long time. Or like a tree: when the roots are planted firmly in the ground, the tree grows steadily and strong, producing healthy fruit and flowers. Think seriously about this.

Perhaps one of the most wonderful lamas of our contemporary age is His Holiness the Dalai Lama, whom Lama Kyabje Zopa Rinpoche reveres as an emanation of the Compassion Buddha, Chenrezig (see Chapter 5). Speak to anyone who has ever been in the presence of His Holiness and they will describe the aura of purity and goodness that emanates from him. He appears so humble and ordinary, so approachable and full of happiness, and yet the

A modern thangka painting showing Lama Tsongkhapa (left), Shakyamuni Buddha (center), and His Holiness the Dalai Lama (right).

world knows the sufferings he has had to endure on behalf of his people. Yet he is unswerving in his conviction that violence and animosity are not the way to deal with problems. The Dalai Lama truly exhibits all the qualities of the Compassion Buddha.

Let me share with you a story that I heard about the Dalai Lama. Once, when he was teaching in America, one of the questions posed to him was :"You must be a most highly realized person. Some say you are the Buddha Chenrezig – can you confirm this?" And His Holiness replied, "I am but a humble monk." Hearing this, the questioner replied sadly, "If that is all you are, then what hope is there for the rest of us? How can we ever reach the state of high realization – let alone enlightenment – if you, such a high being, are still only a humble monk?"

Seeing the genuine dejection in the eyes of the student, His Holiness seemed to reflect for a moment before saying, "Well, sometimes when I contemplate, it seems that I remember the time I drove the chariot that took Buddha on the tour of the city ... the time he met up with old age, sickness, and death ..."

That was as much as His Holiness said on the subject, and those of us who heard this story have often wondered how many other high lamas once lived with the Buddha in Bodhgaya and were among those who attained enlightenment under his teaching.

2

To find happiness and avoid suffering

We should learn about those factors that bring

happiness so we can practice them,

And those factors that bring about suffering,

So we can avoid them.

LAMA KYABJE ZOPA RINPOCHE

Five Tantric Buddhas for Spiritual Transformation

The Dhyani Families

In mystical Buddhism there are five buddha families in the cosmos, led by five transcendent buddhas, or tathagatas, who symbolize the purity of the five associations of body and mind (form, feeling, recognition, consciousness, and conformation, or compound aggregates).

These are the Dhyani buddhas (exalted ones) who preside over the five elements, the five directions, the five colors, and the five wisdoms. They manifest the vitality of Buddhism transcending space and time. These cosmic buddhas have distinct appearances and colors, but we can also think of them as separate manifestations of the one Buddha, each representing an aspect of the total experience of enlightenment that are involved in spiritual transformation.

In the abstract, we can imagine these buddhas taking form in response to the meditative creativity of Buddha's disciples and, over the centuries, becoming popular images for enlightenment. Like white light refracting through faceted crystals to produce a rainbow of colors, so from the single white light of Buddha comes a spectrum of hues, which imbues each of the Dhyani buddhas with attributes that give existence to humankind.

Traditionally, when you have been initiated to Tantric Buddhism (a branch of Mahayana Buddhism), you enter into the mandala (here meaning a sacred palace) of one of the Dhyani buddhas or deities who are in the type of one of five. In Highest Yoga Tantra you also take what are known as the "samaya vows" which transcends your attitude toward the guru and which keeps your attitude pure – not separable from the guru who is giving the initiation. These vows are repeated six times daily in a practice known as the six-session guru yoga – recited three times in the morning and three times in the evening.

Six session guru yoga contains the samaya of the Five Dhyani buddhas and through the practice of six-session guru yoga it causes to achieve the tantra path, method and wisdom, which purifies the five impure aggregates and the purity of each aggregate manifested as the five types of Buddha. As there are doctors who are specialists in dealing with cancer and different types of sickness, these five Dhyani buddhas help overcome these five delusions, which makes us sentient beings suffer. By ceasing these five delusions you can achieve wisdom. When you achieve the five wisdoms you can achieve the five buddhas as well.

The Dhyani buddhas are always shown in meditation pose and are sometimes referred to as buddhas in meditation. In Nepal they adorn many stupas. These four forms are inset around a small shrine at Bhaktapur, Nepal.

THE DHYANI BUDDHAS AS FIVE SYMBOLS OF PURIFICATION

1. Purified ignorance causes it to cease in our consciousness. Purified ignorance manifests as Buddha Vairochana.
2. Overcoming, or purifying, anger and aversion manifests as Buddha Akshobhya.
3. Purified pride and miserliness manifests as Buddha Ratnasambhava.
4. Purified jealousy manifests as Buddha Amoghasiddhi.
5. When the delusion of attachment is purified, this manifests as Buddha Amitabha, the Buddha of Infinite Light.

Meeting the five Dhyani buddhas implies the start of a spiritual journey, which always begins with purification.

Tantric Buddhism and the root guru

Tantric Buddhism requires considerable commitment and thought, plus the guidance of a teacher – someone to whom you initially relate as a virtuous friend, and who then becomes your all-important "tantric guru" when you take Tantric initiation from him. It is he who guides you to your deepest spiritual practices, bringing you to liberation from the cycle of samsara and eventually leading you to perfect enlightenment. Taking a guru implies a renunciation of non-virtuous actions, such as killing and stealing. Above all, it implies embracing the bodhisattva's way of life. This means developing bodhichitta – an intense compassion for the suffering of all beings, which in turn leads to the strong desire to attain enlightenment in order to bring that suffering to an end.

Tantra thus centers on your guru. You can take teachings and even initiations from different gurus, but you only ever have one root guru who is your main guide. Although all Buddhist traditions can be traced back to the same historical Buddha, there are gross and subtle differences in the various lineages, so it is best to find one guru with whom you feel a real affinity. Once you decide to take refuge with him, you should practice intense loyalty, devotion, and obedience to your guru. All traditions, however, say the same thing: the guru is the root of the path, the source of all your goodness, the cause of all your happiness.

The root guru is so central to Buddhist spiritual practice that if you are to make any progress at all, in terms of achieving "realization," you must practice guru yoga. This is done by visualizing your root guru as encompassing all the buddhas, and having the aspect of whichever deity you are practicing. No matter how many hundreds of thousands of buddhas you get to know, progress along the graduated path to enlightenment simply cannot happen unless you receive the blessings of your guru. So when you visualize a whole sky full of buddhas and lamas – what is referred to as "the meditation of the merit field" (see page 40) – it is vital to understand that all of them are manifestations of your gurus.

Therefore the real meaning of the guru is that he encompasses the holy mind of all the buddhas purest consciousness, the mind is the experience of the highest complete bliss. This is referred to as Dharmakaya. Thus it is said that when enlightenment is attained, the mind instantly understands this and becomes one with all the buddhas.

So a guru (or Tantric master, if you are taking Tantric initiations from him) is someone whom you should be very careful about taking on. You should check him out thoroughly, feel that you really want to study under him, and revere him as a true spiritual master before committing yourself to the samaya vows.

This book merely points the way. I am simply planting a seed in your mind, sharing what I have learned and experienced, and what I have discovered to be truly awesome. I am not a qualified teacher, but having known and benefited so much from my guru, it is possible for me to open some windows for you.

Lama Lhundrup Khen Rinpoche, the Abbot of Kopan Monastery, Nepal. His guru is Lama Yeshe, whose teachings are the basis of the Yeshe Program at Kopan, where around 360 monks and nuns now study. The monastery was first established in 1971 following Lama Lhundrup's escape from China in 1959 with His Holiness the Dalai Lama.

THE MERIT FIELD MEDITATION

Meditating on the Buddha merit field is an excellent way of practicing guru devotion. The practitioner begins by considering their root guru as the absolute guru – the Dharmakaya – the unity of all the buddhas' holy minds. A painting of the merit field is visualized, with the root guru sitting in the center of the sky (see right). He manifests as Shakyamuni Buddha, who is called Tubwang; and as as Vajradhara, the buddha at the heart of Tubwang. Vajradhara is the embodiment of all the gurus.

Now one being is visualized: the lama, the guru, one aspect. This is the absolute guru, who manifests as a conventional guru to guide a person to enlightenment. The guru is also visualized as all the lineage lamas, who send their blessings.

Visualized on the right side of the picture is Maitreya Buddha, the buddha of loving kindness (see Chapter 9) and all his lineage lamas and disciples. On the left, Manjushri, the Buddha of wisdom, is visualized, with all his lineage lamas and disciples.

By manifesting thus, the guru guides the practitioner from one happiness to another happiness and ultimately to enlightenment. Now s/he thinks:

My guru also appears as all the lineage lamas of the old Kadampa traditions, which start with Lama Atisha* to guide me from happiness to happiness to enlightenment.

Then my guru appears as all the lineage lamas of the new Kadampa traditions, including Tsongkhapa, to guide me from happiness to happiness to enlightenment.

My guru manifests as the direct gurus surrounding Shakyamuni Buddha/Vajradhara, and as the tantric deities Highest Yoga tantra, Yoga tantra, Charya tantra, and Kriya tantra to guide me from happiness to happiness to enlightenment.

My guru manifests as the 1,000 buddhas of this fortunate eon, including the thirty-five Confession buddhas and the Medicine buddhas to guide me from happiness to happiness to enlightenment.

My guru also appears as the bodhisattvas like the sixteen arhats, dakas (the male equivalent of dakinis), dakinis (fairy maidens), and Dharma protectors, to guide me from happiness to happiness to enlightenment.

*a renowned eleventh-century Indian Buddhist master

The Buddha merit field is the visualization of a skyful of buddhas and lamas, with one's root guru at the center.

The Five Dhyani buddhas

The richness of imagery and the wealth of symbolism associated with the Dhyani buddhas struck a chord within me when I first came to know about them. Although they can be depicted in the humble robes of the historical Buddha, Shakyamuni (see chapter 1), these cosmic buddhas often appear in jewel-encrusted robes, with crowns and ornaments. The mandalas of the Dhyani buddhas are especially engaging.

You can get to know the Dhyani buddhas intellectually and visually first, and then allow your mind and heart to connect with each one individually, for different aspects of the enlightenment experience. You may be especially taken by the incorporation of elements, colors, symbols, mudras, and directions in their imagery.

The Dhyani buddhas can be viewed as spiritual kings who preside over their respective mandalas. Each one can be pictured in his Pure Land, overseeing different realms and directions, and helping sentient beings to overcome particular afflictions with his special wisdom.

THE DHYANI BUDDHA VISUALIZATIONS

A visualization is presented for each Dhyani buddha, in the caption accompanying their thangka images – see pages 45, 49, 51, 53, and 55. Before each visualization, the person practicing performs this preliminary meditation.

First, one feels that their mind purifies into emptiness. The mind, understanding this emptinenss, then transforms into Guru Shakyamuni Buddha, with one face, two arms, and a gold-colored body. His face is extremely beautiful, with a loving smile and compassionate eye. Every second, every pore of his holy body radiates numberless buddhas to sentient beings, liberating them from suffering and bringing them to liberation and enlightenment.

Guru Shakyamuni's mantra is chanted: Tayata Om Mune, Mune, Maha Muneye Soha, followed by the visualization for one or more of the Dhyani buddhas.

A Dhyani (meditation) buddha inset into the stupa at Boudhanath, Nepal.

BUDDHA AKSHOBHYA

Although Buddha Akshobhya (who is blue in color) is usually visualized in the center of Dhyani buddha mandalas, sometimes he is transferred to the east and Vairochana comes to the center. Many lineages regard Akshobhya as the most important of the Dhyani buddhas because, of the five aggregates, the aggregate of consciousness can be regarded as the most important in our spiritual journey.

Askhobhya also manifests as Buddha Mitrugpa. The Buddha Mitrugpa mantra practice (see pages 46–47) is said to be extremely powerful for "rescuing" those who have fallen into the lower realms of existence (see page 62–63). Akshobhya is depicted touching the earth with his right hand and holding an upright vajra (thunderbolt) in his left hand. Touching the earth recalls the moment when Shakyamuni Buddha overcame the Mara and the earth goddess was called forth to bear witness to Buddha having practiced the Six Perfections (see page 12), thereby qualifying him to attain enlightenment. The element of Buddha Akshobhya is water, and the chakra (energy center) associated with him is the heart chakra.

Akshobhya is the lord of the Tathagata family. This buddha manifests Dharma, transforming hatred and aversion into the transcendental wisdom of the sphere of the Dharma. Among the other powerful Buddhas of the Tathagata family are Buddha Vajrasattva and Buddha Vajrapani.

Akshobhya's blessings enable us to develop the wisdom that understands the true nature of reality. This is often referred to as becoming awakened and overcoming ignorance.

Here is the visualization of Buddha Akshobhya: Nectar beams come from Buddha Akshobhya, purifying anger. Where there is violence, war is stopped and everyone generates loving kindness, patience, and the whole path to enlightenment. The transcendental wisdom of Dharmadhatu is actualized in their minds and in the minds of all sentient beings.

THE SPECIAL PRACTICE OF BUDDHA AKSHOBHYA

There is a powerful deity of purification called Mitrukpa who is a manifestation of Akshobhya. There are tremendous benefits to be had from reciting his mantra and even seeing his image or mantra written.

One of the most memorable summaries of the benefits of reciting the Mitrugpa mantra was given by the Venerable Ribur Rinpoche, one of Lama Kyabje Zopa Rinpoche's gurus, when he visited Singapore in 1997. Already in his eighties, Ribur Rinpoche remains as sprightly and cheerful as ever. Reciting the Mitrugpa mantra, he says:

- Purifies all negativities accumulated in past lives
- Prevents the ripening of past negative actions
- Purifies the five extreme negatives of killing your mother, killing your father, killing an arhat (a saint), causing a buddha to shed blood, and causing disharmony among the spiritual community of monks or nuns
- Purifies all inauspicious signs arising from negative actions
- Has the power to reverse untimely death
- Prevents all those who hear it (animals and humans) from falling into the three lower realms (the animal realm, the hungry ghosts realm, and the hell realm)
- Has the power to rescue anyone who has been dead a long time from the hell realm, if you recite it 100,000 times and dedicate it to that person
- Has the power to prevent any corpse that may be one week old from being reborn in any of the three lower realms, if it is recited 100,000 times over sand, sesame seed, or flour, which is then sprinkled on the head of the dead person
- Has the power to purify all negative karma, thereby protecting a person from entering the lower realms, even if they have committed very heavy karma – if, while dying or at the instant of death, they see the mantra in written form.

BUDDHA MITRUGPA'S DAILY MANTRA

NAMO RATNA TRAYAYA
OM KAMKANI KAMKANI
ROTSANI ROTSANI TROTANI TROTANI
TRASANI TRASANI TRATIHANA TRATIHANA
SARWA KARMA PARAM PARANI ME
SARWA SATO NENTSA SOHA

For as long as space endures

And for as long as living beings remain

Until then may I too abide

To dispel the misery of the world

SHANTIDEVA

BUDDHA RATNASAMBHAVA

The mandala of Buddha Ratnasambhava (who is yellow in color) is in the southern direction. The word ratna means "jewel," and Ratnasambhava can be regarded as the wish-fulfilling jewel. He signifies Dharma transforming pride, miserliness, and avarice into the wisdom of equanimity. His identifying mudra (sacred hand gesture) is the gesture of supreme giving, with his right hand extended downward, palm outward. His left hand rests on his lap, sometimes holding a beautiful jewel. His clan is the Ratna family, so the symbol of Ratnasambhava is the jewel. He is associated with transforming a poverty mentality into a wealth mentality. The element of Buddha Ratnasambhava is earth, and his chakra is the navel chakra.

He is best visualized as continuously distributing spiritual wealth and jewels over the universe, with no thought of ever running out, for it seems he has a bottomless reservoir of spiritual riches. His Pure Land flows with abundance and he is "wealthy beyond greed." So Ratnasambhava practice makes your own mind an endless source of riches. The Wealth buddhas (known as Jambhalas, see Chapter 8) belong to Ratnasambhava's family and, reflecting the generous mentality of this buddha clan, are viewed as endless benefactors.

Ratnasambhava's blessings give us the potential
to overcome pride and miserliness,
thereby developing inner calm.

Here is the visualization of Buddha Ratnasambhava: From the jewels of Ratnasambhava, everyone receives what they want, what they need; including wealth, teachers, and teachings. A transcendental wisdom of equanimity arises, causing them to become enlightened like Buddha Ratnasambhava. Nectar beams are visualized emitting from Ratnasambhava, purifying the disease of miserliness, which does not allow you to enjoy yourself even though you are rich. This is a painful, unhappy mind; now you can achieve so much happiness up to enlightenment by using your wealth to create merit.

BUDDHA AMITABHA

The mandala of Buddha Amitabha (who is red in color) is in the western direction. Amitabha is the Buddha of Infinite Light, and he represents the Dharma transforming the afflictions of lust and desire into discriminating wisdom. He is thus the buddha who purifies the delusion of attachment.

Generally, like all of the five tathagatas, Amitabha sits in the lotus posture, with his hands in the mudra of meditative contemplation; sometimes he holds a begging bowl. He is lord of the Lotus family, and his symbol is the red lotus of compassion. The lotus is a special Buddhist symbol, signifying gentleness and purity, and buddhas are always depicted sitting on a lotus flower. Amitabha is probably the best known Dhyani buddha.

The paradise of Amitabha is known as the western paradise, or Sukhavati (in Tibetan, Dewachen, meaning Great Happiness Pure Land), and it is believed that in accordance with a vow that he made prior to attaining enlightenment, you have only to recite Amitabha's name to be reborn into his realm, thereby attaining enlightenment through what is described as "the light of Amitabha's great compassion." His element is the all-consuming fire that has the power to burn all of our delusions, and especially the terrible delusion of attachment. His chakra is the throat chakra.

Amitabha Buddha is widely worshipped and revered in China, Korea, and Japan where Pure Land Buddhism is practiced. Devotees believe that reciting his mantra will cause their rebirth in the western paradise, where conditions are conducive to the eventual attainment of enlightenment. Here they take teachings from Amitabha himself, and from all the other buddhas who reside in the same paradise land. Two beloved goddesses of Amitabha's Pure Land family are the goddess of mercy, Kuan Yin – who is the Chinese form of the Compassion Buddha, Chenrezig (see Chapter 5) – and Green Tara (see Chapter 7) who is said to have been born from the tears of the Compassion Buddha. There are detailed sadhanas (meditative practices) that are believed by practitioners of Pure Land Buddhism to enable them to visualize the western paradise so vividly that it becomes real.

Amitabha's blessings develop within us the potential for compassion, which arises from overcoming the delusion of attachment.

Here is the visualization of Buddha Amitabha: From Amitabha, nectar beams are emitted, purifying all attachment and sufferings that come from desire, such as relationship problems, craving, addiction, a dissatisfied mind, fear, quarrels, wars and so forth. Everyone actualizes renunciation and discerning wisdom, thus becoming Buddha Amitabha.

BUDDHA AMOGHASIDDHI

The mandala of Buddha Amoghasiddhi (who is green in color) is in the northern direction. This is the tathagata who symbolizes unobstructed success. He is the buddha of the world of politicians, kings, and ambitious people – those who are perpetually jealous of others, who are competitive to a fault, and whose sole purpose in life is to wind up getting more: more wealth, more success, and more power. When you need to operate in this kind of unscrupulous world, call on this vivid green buddha.

Amoghasiddhi's mudra signifies fearlessness and protection: his right hand is held with its palm facing outward in the "fear not" gesture, at the level of the Buddha's heart, with the fingers pointing skyward. This mudra is one of command and authority. His left hand is in the contemplation mudra. It is said that simply thinking of his image causes your fears to vanish instantly. His green-colored body is also extremely soothing. The path of Amoghasiddhi is the path that overcomes fear. He is also the buddha of action, so we can visualize him as the tathagata who inspires strong yang energy, who practices spontaneous bodhichitta and is completely compassionate. His element is wind (air), and his chakra is the base chakra.

Amoghasiddhi represents the Dharma transforming envy and jealousy into all-accomplishing wisdom. He is the head of the Karma family, and his symbol is the double or crossed vajra (thunderbolt, or diamond scepter). The single vajra is the powerful thunderbolt that can cut through everything; the crossed vajra has all this intense power doubled.

Amoghasiddhi gives us the potential to develop fearlessness, which results from overcoming jealousy.

Here is the visualization of Buddha Amoghasiddhi: From him come nectar beams that purify the agony of jealousy, the mind made unhappy by seeing others' enjoyment; that which brings torment and unrest in this life and in future lives, causing many problems in the world. Everyone develops the mind that takes great joy in the wealth, power, position, good fortune, and enjoyment of others; they receive the all-accomplishing transcendental wisdom, and become enlightened in the aspect of Buddha Amoghasiddhi.

BUDDHA VAIROCHANA

The mandala of Buddha Vairochana (who is white in color) is generally in the eastern realm (although occasionally in the center), and he is known as the great illuminator, the great sun.

His mudra is the Dharmachakra mudra, that of teaching, also known as the turning of the wheel. Both hands are held at chest level, with the left hand facing inward. The index finger and thumb of each hand touch to make a circle. His symbol is the golden wheel, suggesting benevolent kingship. The element of this tathagata is water, and he is associated with the crown chakra.

Vairochana belongs to the Vajra family. The vajra, or diamond scepter (thunderbolt) is a powerful emblem of sovereignty – it has the indestructible qualities of the diamond, able to overcome anything that crosses its path. Vairochana helps in overcoming the affliction of ignorance which is the root of samsara.

Vairochana gives us the potential to develop balance and wisdom, which results from overcoming anger and aversion.

Here is the visualization of Buddha Vairochana:
From him come nectar beams, purifying ignorance, the root of samsara: ignorance of ultimate nature, not knowing what is right or wrong. Sufferings continue for aeons until one removes the root of suffering, which is ignorance. Nectar beams purify all ignorance; everyone receives the mirror-like transcendental wisdom, and becomes enlightened in the form of Buddha Vairochana.

3

If you plant a seed in the desert, even though it is planted in soil, it is so hot that it may get cooked, and it won't grow. In the same way, by making purification and creating merit, our negativities become like seeds planted without water.

LAMA KYABJE ZOPA RINPOCHE

Purifying Negativity:

Vajrasattva and the thirty-five Confession Buddhas

Purifying the mind

All minds require spiritual cleansing and purification. Negative blocks that have built up over time leave plenty of negative karma, which is the cause of having to endure illness, pain, and all kinds of obstacles that bring with them suffering, loss, and death. These negativities are carried as invisible baggage from past lives in our consciousness. They follow us from lifetime to lifetime and, when conditions cause them to "ripen," that is when we experience suffering. In this life we have secured – against all the odds – a miraculous rebirth in the human realm (see overleaf), where we are able to do the most to cleanse and purify our karmic score card. Lama Kyabje Zopa Rinpoche says:

How do we solve life's problems – failure in business, obstacles in a job; how do we find happiness and avoid sickness, live a long life, always have a friend that does exactly as we wish, have people to support us, listen to us, not criticize us, praise us, serve us, help us whenever we need help, and have all the comforts?

You can achieve this in two ways.

This is the first way: because all obstacles, the undesirable things in life, come from negative karma, you can do purification practice every day. This way, you don't need to suffer or experience the problems that are the result of negative karma.

The second way is to abstain from creating negative karma again – by living in morality, which results in happiness in this life and in all future lives. Purifying negative karma and creating good karma are both Dharma practice. So whatever lifestyle you have, you need to practice Dharma twenty-four hours a day. This means keeping your mind healthy, positive, pure, and virtuous.

For this, we need the help of the Purification buddhas: Vajrasattva and the thirty-five Confession buddhas.

The thirty-five Confession buddhas are visualized as part of purification practice in five groups, which relate to the five families of Dhyani buddhas.

SIX WAYS TO PURIFY NEGATIVE KARMA

Buddha's teachings on the path to enlightenment speak of six methods that we can use to purify negative karma:

1. Reading the sutra texts (for example, the Diamond Cutter or the Perfection of Wisdom)
2. Meditating on emptiness
3. Reciting special powerful mantras
4. Making holy objects, such as the miniature Buddha images known as tsa-tsas, stupas, or paintings
5. Making offerings to holy objects
6. Reciting the names of powerful buddhas, such as Vajrasattva and the thirty-five Confession buddhas.

Any one, or a combination, of these six methods can be used to purify eons of negative karma. Over time, if you pursue the spiritual path, you will certainly find yourself doing all of them at some stage of your journey.

Every happiness you experience in every moment is caused by past good karma; and every suffering you experience every moment is caused by past bad karma. And every moment thought and action, depending on whether it is positive or negative, produces happiness or suffering.

LAMA KYABJE ZOPA RINPOCHE

THE SIX REALMS OF EXISTENCE

The Six Realms of Existence describe different "worlds," representing different kinds of samsaric suffering.

1. *The hell (narak) realms*
    The realms of greatest suffering
2. *The hungry ghost (preta) realm*
    The realm of intense suffering of hunger and thirst
3. *The animal realm*
    The realm of extensive suffering of ignorance
4. *The demi-god (asura) realm*
    The realm of material pleasures
5. *The god realm*
    The realm of exclusive enjoyment
6. *The human realm*
    The realm of most precious rebirth

The hell realm, the realm of the hungry ghosts, and the animal realm comprise the three lower realms. The three upper realms are: the demi-god realm, the god realm, and the human realm. Rebirth in the lower realms represents the fully ripened dire consequences of negative karma (see page 60) caused by negative actions of body, speech, and mind. Those in the upper realms can help by dedicating prayers to those who have passed on to the lower realms otherwise, the suffering is expressed until the cause is exhausted.

THE HELL (NARAK) REALMS

These are the realms with the greatest experience of suffering such as intense burning heat or unbearable cold. The suffering is so great that it appears to last for an extreme length of time.

THE HUNGRY GHOST (PRETA) REALM

In this realm the main suffering is excruciating hunger and thirst with no respite. There is constant fear and exhaustion.

THE ANIMAL REALM

Here the chief suffering is ignorance. In the animal kingdom there is also the suffering of hunger and thirst; of being threatened by natural enemies; of being exploited by human beings for flesh and for work.

When the mind is tranquil, you are resting. When your mind is excited with attachment, it is hallucinating, obscuring, or tormenting. Living in morality, with a positive, healthy mind, causes your mental continuum to be peaceful and happy.

LAMA KYABJE ZOPA RINPOCHE

THE DEMI-GOD (ASURA) REALM

In the realm of demi-gods there are rich material pleasures. Demi-gods are said to envy those residing in the god realms, so they suffer from jealousy and quarreling. In this realm there is no motivation to meditate or to practice Dharma. Those in the demi-god realm can live in luxury for eons, but there comes a time when only negative karma is left on their karmic score card, and this propels them into a rebirth in one of the lower realms.

THE GOD REALM

The god realm is preoccupied with enjoyment — with bodies of light, transcendental nectar, long life, and so on. They neither see nor recognize suffering so it is very hard for them to practice Dharma. When the positive karma to be born in this realm is exhausted they suffer intensely at the time of death, seeing that they will lose everything and no virtue has been accumulated, must fall to a lower realm.

THE HUMAN REALM

The human realm is also one of suffering — where disease, aging, and death are inevitable. However, human rebirth can be the most precious of all in the cycle of samsaric existence. Rebirth as a human being enables the practice of Dharma, the reciting of mantras, and spiritual practices that hold the key to liberation from samsara. It is only here that the mind can be controlled and the wisdom of emptiness and compassion realized.

Retreat at Kopan in the Kathmandu valley

Soon after meeting Lama Kyabje Zopa Rinpoche, I participated in a meditation retreat at Kopan monastery in the Kathmandu valley. This is Rinpoche's own monastery, perched on a small hill just above the famous Boudhanath stupa, with the Himalayan mountains rising behind it. Here, for over twenty years, Rinpoche's monks and nuns have been conducting an annual month-long meditation course from November to December. Organized as a spiritual retreat, it includes in its curriculum the taking of precepts or vows, keeping silence, and daily purification practices. The cost of the course (including accommodation and meals) is minimal, for it is not a profit-making venture. Students come from all over the world to participate, and for as long as it has been in existence the program has been heavily oversubscribed. Participants get to know about it by word of mouth, and each year many people have to be placed on the waiting list. In the last week of the course Lama Kyabje Zopa Rinpoche himself arrives at Kopan to give teachings and initiations.

I had been told that the experience would be a life-changing one, but was also warned that it would be difficult. Facilities are quite basic, although in reality they are "luxurious" when compared to the way in which Buddhists of other eras used to learn. And going through purification is never easy, for the practices speed up the ripening of negative karma – albeit in a less severe way. So it is not uncommon to fall ill, feel depressed, and generally become impatient. Purification does not completely take away suffering. Instead it speeds up its manifestation and makes it bearable. And afterwards there is a real sense of release. Life becomes clearer and all that is good within you – especially your latent compassionate heart – begins to flower, while all that is bad begins to fade.

At Kopan we recited the Vajrasattva purification mantras each evening before retiring for the night, and did 108 prostrations to the thirty-five Confession buddhas each morning before sunrise.

Kopan itself is incredibly beautiful. It is like being in heaven: a paradise land where clouds nudge at your feet in the early mornings just before the sun rises. The air is very brisk and clean. All around there seems to be a light mist, and in the distance are the majestic peaks of the Himalayan mountains. From the main gompa (prayer hall) come the sounds of monks chanting as they do their early morning pujas (religious offerings). In the treetops, prayer flags flutter in the gentle breeze, sending waves of blessings into the valley below.

The whole place persuades the mind to settle, grow calm, and feel gentle. In the beginning the experience is difficult, especially since, being December, it is also very cold in the Kathmandu valley. Soon, however, the body transcends these aspects of physical discomfort and engages the spirit, and then it becomes rather magical.

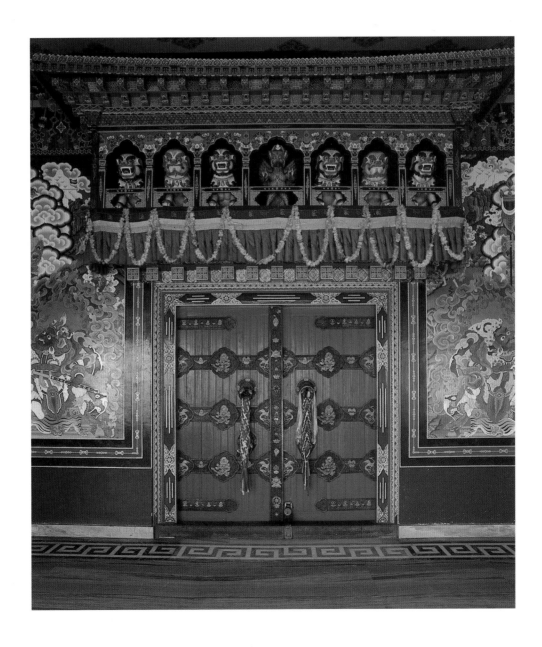

Seven Dharma protectors sit above the main door of Kopan monastery, Nepal, which protect against the nadas, or obscurations of the mind.

The Buddha of Purification: Vajrasattva

In Kopan I was introduced to Vajrasattva, the Buddha of Purification, who is gloriously beautiful, tantalizingly mysterious, and esoteric. He has a white body, which suggests the supreme essence of all the buddhas. He is a cosmic buddha, who is depicted both alone and in a tight embrace with his consort. Vajrasattva is visualized as a royal celestial buddha, wearing a crown studded with jewels and with an aura of five colored lights – red, blue, yellow, green, and white – around his head. This signifies the union of the five Dhyani tathagatas (see Chapter 2), so Vajrasattva embodies all of their combined wisdom.

Vajrasattva sits serenely in the diamond posture. His right hand holds a vajra (thunderbolt) at his heart, symbolizing his skilful means, while his left hand holds the vajra handle of a bell, resting on his left thigh at his hip, signifying wisdom. Sometimes both hands are shown crossed at his heart. The two symbols of Vajrasattva – the thunderbolt and the bell – are like the yin and yang of the enlightenment experience; the union of method and wisdom, compassion and emptiness.

Practicing Vajrasattva's purification is extremely potent and his sadhana (meditation visualization) can easily be incorporated into daily life. This is a simply way to reconnect with the inner nature. Without Vajrasattva's purification it seems as if we are wandering the world – lost, alone, and abjectly poor – when in reality we are as rich as anything. The key to unlocking the spiritual wealth within us lies in Vajrasattva's hundred-syllable mantra (see page 72). Practicing Vajrasattva's sadhana and reciting his mantra twenty-eight times, just once a day, can purify inconceivable eons of negative karma. The mantra is one that devotees of both Mahayana and Tantric Buddhism chant continuously as part of their daily purification practice.

It is said that anyone wishing to start on the quick path to enlightenment – the diamond path of Tantric Buddhism – is expected by their spiritual guru to have completed four preliminaries, one of which is reciting Vajrasattva's mantra 100,000 times. It takes about three months to do this, if you are on retreat and faithfully doing four sessions a day. Otherwise, such an aspiration could take up to a year to complete.

Vajrasattva's body is pure milk-white, and adorned with the finest jewels, ornaments, gemstones, and silken garments. The essence of this buddha is concentrated purity that reflects the strength and power of a clear, light consciousness.

There is no need to get stressed about this. I have tried several times to fulfil the Vajrasattva commitment and have failed miserably. Once I was part of a group doing the Vajrasattva retreat in California with Lama Kyabje Zopa Rinpoche, in his meditation center in the redwood forests, known as Land of the Medicine Buddha. Alas, my feeble mind gave up. I have yet to complete the requisite number of mantras, but I like to think of Vajrasattva in his great compassion accepting my laziness as part of me. He knows that I am practically crawling along the path to enlightenment, so he helps me along. Despite my inadequate practice, I am convinced that he answers my prayers.

When I first came upon the visage of Vajrasattva, in the form of a thangka painting, I was bowled over by the sheer beauty of this buddha. And when I learned his hundred-syllable mantra, I found it surprisingly easy to memorize. Then I found myself reciting it under my breath daily, weekly, and monthly, until it is now a subconscious part of my waking moments. It is sweetly seductive. It embraces me and, in so doing, cleanses away karmic dirt, which prevents me from seeing clearly.

Slowly I realize that as the dirty surface that makes me "sleep" – the sleep of ignorance, making me blind to the true nature of existence – dissolves, so my mind becomes clearer, brighter, and more focussed. It goes something like this … Say you cannot read small print, because in your older years you have come to rely on reading glasses. Seeing words blur in front of you resembles a mind that is not purified of karmic delusions. Once you start to do the Vajrasattva sadhana of purification seriously, it is like suddenly putting on your glasses. Instantly words jump out at you and become crystal-clear. Your mind becomes vigorous and sturdy, wiser, more patient, and a great deal calmer.

As with all meditative practices, it involves preliminaries, visualization, recitation of the mantra, and the dedication. There are different ways to do the Vajrasattva practice and it is best to follow the method that your lama teaches, or to use one with which you are comfortable. The practice takes on greater meaning and substance when you have been empowered to do it by receiving initiation from a qualified lineage lama.

THE PRELIMINARIES

First, the mind is calmed, allowing access to one's deepest nature. Then a feeling of really wanting purification is generated. All accumulated negative actions are contemplated, realizing the heavy load of karmic debts and baggage that are in need of cleansing.

The preliminaries involve a surrender of sorts. They necessitate doing daily practice over a period of time, which eventually adds up to 100,000 repetitions. Four major practices reflect this surrender and renunciation:

The first preliminary involves taking refuge in the Triple Gem – the Buddha, Dharma (the Buddha's teachings), and Sangha (the ordained community of monks and nuns) – which emanate from, and in, the lama or guru. It is excellent to set a time period in which to eventually recite 100,000 times the refuge prayer, as follows:

NAMO GURUBHAY, NAMO BUDDHAYA,
NAMO DHARMAYA, NAMO SANGHAYA.

The second preliminary involves making 100,000 full-length prostrations to all the buddhas of the ten directions. (This prostration practice can also be combined with the refuge practice above, making a prostration to the Triple Gem as the refuge prayer is recited with Vajrasattva mantra or, most commonly, with the Thirty Five Buddhas of Confession Practice.)

The third preliminary involves making mandala offerings (see page 252) to the buddhas of the ten directions. Again, it is excellent to set a goal of eventually doing 100,000 mandala offerings.

The fourth preliminary is the purification of the mind. This usually means setting aside some time and making the effort to do the powerful Vajrasattva practice.

To complete the preliminaries it is a good idea to go on a retreat in order to finish chanting Vajrasattva's mantra 100,000 times.

VISUALIZATION AND RECITATION OF THE MANTRA

The practitioner visualizes Vajrasattva seated on an open white lotus on a moon disk above their head. He is white, translucent, and adorned with beautiful ornaments and clothes. His right hand holds a vajra, symbolic of great bliss, at his heart; his left hand holds a bell, symbolic of the wisdom of emptiness, at his left hip. These two attributes signify his attainment of the unified state of enlightenment. At Vajrasattva's heart, on a moon disk, is the seed-syllable HUM, and the letters of his hundred-syllable mantra run clockwise around its edge.

From the HUM at Vajrasattva's heart, light radiates in all directions, asking the buddhas to bestow their blessings. They send white rays of light and nectar, which are absorbed into the HUM and the letters of the mantra at Vajrasattva's heart. They fill his whole body, enhancing the magnificence of his appearance and the brilliance of his mantra. The following hundred-syllable mantra is recited twenty-one times:

OM VAJRASATTVA SAMAYA MANU PALAYA
VAJRASATTVA DENOPA TITA, DIDO MAY BHAWA,
SUTO KAYO MAY BHAWA, SUPO KAYO MAY BHAWA
ANU RAKTO MAY BHAWA

SARWA SIDDHI MAY PRAYATSA,
   SARWA KARMA SU TSA MAY
TSITAM SHRIYAM KURU HUM, HA HA HA HA HO
BHAGAWAN – SARWA TATAGATA,
   VAJRA MA MAY MUNTSA
VAJRA BHAWA, MAHA SAMAYA SATTVA
AH HUM PEY

Vajra refers to the unshakable, thunderbolt-like quality of enlightened wisdom that cannot be destroyed; Sattva means one who possesses the very essence of the indestructible knowledge of wisdom. When there is not enough time, the short mantra, Om Vajrasattva Hum, can be recited twenty-eight times. While reciting either of the mantras, the flow of light and nectar is visualized, cleansing the body of all negativities, obscurations, and obstructions.

Vajrasattva is a cosmic or celestial buddha. He represents the total wisdom of all five Dhyani buddhas (see Chapter 2).

GENERATING A FEELING OF REGRET

In order to purify it is important to generate a healing regret, a purifying regret. Since here is a method to purify negstive karma, regret is not just torturing onself. There is a method so one must do that and the way to do that is to purify with the four opponent powers.

With deep regret, the specific negativities to be purified are remembered. This might be losing one's temper, telling lies, breaking a spiritual vow, or being irritable with a family member. The negativity may be large or small: as small as killing a mosquito or, occasionally, as serious as murdering someone. Whatever the particular non-virtuous action, it is meditated upon deeply and with great remorse. A person then thinks the following:

> *The negative karma I have accumulated from beginningless time is as extensive as the ocean. I know each negative action leads to countless eons of suffering, yet I am constantly creating nothing but negative actions. I try to avoid non-virtue and to practice positive acts, yet day and night, without respite, negativity and moral downfalls come to me like rainfall. I lack the ability to purify these faults and, with these negative imprints in my mind, I could suddenly die and find myself falling to an unfortunate rebirth. Please, Vajrasattva, with your great compassion, guide me from such misery.*

Three visualizations are then practiced while reciting the mantra:

PURIFYING DOWN: Imagining that all the negativities of body, speech, and mind are being flushed out by the light and nectar that flows downward through the body. Imagining all negative karma, obscurations, and illness leaving the lower part of the body in the form of filthy liquid. Feeling strongly that they no longer exist, and that one is completely purified and overcome with blissful energy.

PURIFYING UP: Imagining the light and nectar filling the body. Starting from below, visualizing that all negativities rise and overflow through the upper openings of the body. Feeling that they no longer exist, and that one is completely cleansed and purified, filled with great blissful spiritual energy.

INSTANTANEOUS PURIFICATION: A tremendous forceful stream of light and nectar energy explodes from Vajrasattva, filling the entire body instantly. Negative karma and obscurations vanish completely. They no longer exist; the body and mind are completely and instantly purified, and are filled with great blissful energy.

These three visualizations can be done individually, or practiced consecutively in the same meditation session. As they are visualized strongly, there is a conviction that even the most subtle obscurations and shadows, which prevent an understanding the true nature of existence, disappear. A person doing these visualizations must feel that this purification opens their eyes and awakens them from the sleep of ignorance.

Next, a silent promise in the heart is made to Vajrasattva, specifying a period of time during which this promise will be kept: *"I shall not create any of these negativities of body, speech, and mind from now until _____."* It is best to specify a twenty-four hour period; this is not being overly ambitious, and enables the negativities that have become a habit to be worked through.

Vajrasattva is extremely pleased and replies, *"My spiritual child of the essence, all your negativities, obscurations, and degenerate vows are completely purified."*

A delighted Vajrasattva is visualized. He melts into light and dissolves into the person who visualizes him. Body, speech, and mind become inseparably one with Vajrasattva's holy body, speech, and mind. This is a vital part of the sadhana; feeling the buddha dissolving into the human body, a person immediately becomes the pure essence of the buddha.

This feeling is savored. It is a blissful experience, and this visualization is one of the most powerful practices, especially if the mantras are recited with great focus and concentration. Like all prayers, this prayer must be heartfelt in order to reach the level of consciousness that enables someone to feel at one with Vajrasattva.

The final part of the visualization is the dedication. The spiritual merit that has been gained in attaining the enlightened state of Vajrasattva should be dedicated, so that all beings can be liberated from their suffering. The practitioner wishes that the compassionate heart within them grows and expands, and never wanes.

There are more detailed ways to do the Vajrasattva purification, but I hope that this will be easy for those who have not done the meditation before. Whatever method is followed, as long as it is practiced with the proper motivation, then there is no bad karma, no monolithic negativity that cannot be overcome. But – and this is the key – there must be real belief that the power of this practice can eradicate and purify all negativities. If there is the slightest doubt, then the whole process weakens.

The thirty-five Confession buddhas' visualization

In the center is Guru Shakyamuni Buddha, and at his heart the 1,000-armed Avalokiteshvara (or the four-armed Chenrezig, or whichever aspect is preferred). At the heart of Avalokiteshvara is the seed-syllable HRIH, which is the essence of great compassion inseparable from one's own guru, who is the Dharmakaya of all the buddhas, and manifests in the form of Shakyamuni Buddha.

From the syllable HRIH, the thirty-five Confession buddhas manifest. (Note that, as Guru Shakyamuni is already there, there are just thirty-four more to come.) They are visualized in groups below Guru Shakyamuni: the first line containing six buddhas, and the other lines having seven buddhas each. Each group belongs to the family of one of the five Dhyani buddhas (see page 34):

The first six buddhas should be visualized in the form of the Dhyani buddha Akshobhya.

The second line of seven buddhas should be visualized in the form of the Dhyani buddha Vairochana.

The next seven buddhas should be visualized in the form of the Dhyani buddha Ratnasambhava.

The next seven buddhas should be visualized in the form of the Dhyani buddha Amitabha.

The last seven buddhas should be visualized in the form of the Dhyani buddha, Amoghasiddhi.

A thangka painting showing the thirty-five Confession buddhas, arranged in five rows. At the head of each is the Dhyani buddha that represents each family group.

Prostrations to the thirty-five Confession buddhas

Lama Kyabje Zopa Rinpoche says that negative karma doubles every day when it is not purified. From being very light, it can become very heavy, negative karma. For instance, when we kill a mosquito we don't have a bad conscience, so we do not purify ourselves and do not confess. But after fifteen days, the tiny act of killing that mosquito has expanded so that it is equal to the negative karma of killing a human being – very heavy karma indeed. It is the same with other negativities: for example, the heaviest negative karmas are created with the mind and when this happens, it increases in the same way. So there is a huge need to purify and accumulate merit in order to avoid suffering.

Rinpoche taught me that one of the most vital things to incorporate into my practice was making prostrations to as many holy objects as possible. These include Buddha statues, stupas, and images. I recall very clearly that when he told me about prostrations, he went to great lengths to stress how you should do it correctly, and then the merit and the power of purification will be enormous. If, however, you stay down on the ground too long, you might cause yourself to be reborn as a reptile; if you open your fingers while prostrating, you might be reborn as an animal with webbed feet …

I shook my head: this was a bit much, I thought. "Better not to do it at all – why risk becoming a duck?" I remember saying.

An intrinsic part of Buddhist practice is prostration before a stupa and its circumambulation (walking around it clockwise). This gold stupa is at Swayambhu, Nepal.

Rinpoche was unimpressed with my feeble attempt at humor. He repeated, "It is necessary to do the prostrations," and then proceeded to show me how, asking one of the monks to demonstrate: from the way the fingers are to be placed right through all the steps in making a full-length prostration. The Venerable Jampa, Rinpoche's assistant, demonstrated, and that was how I learned how to do prostrations.

Then Rinpoche told me about the thirty-five Confession buddhas. He advised making three prostrations to each of the buddhas, and saying their names out loud as I did so. He told me to start by taking refuge and reciting the prostration mantra. That was during the first week of my acquaintance with Rinpoche. Already I was flabbergasted. There were so many buddhas – how was I to learn all their names, and how would I be able to pronounce them?

I was relieved to learn later on, when the Venerable Jampa was kind enough to open his prayer notes for me, that it was perfectly acceptable to recite the names of the Confession buddhas in English. Rinpoche also gave me a tip on how to make the practice easier to remember, saying, "One very easy way to visualize the thirty-five buddhas is by dividing them into five groups of seven buddhas each ..."

The best way to get to know the Confession buddhas is to obtain a thangka or picture and become thoroughly familiar with them. They can then be visualized as prostrations to the thirty-five buddhas are made.

Monks perform full prostrations daily in devotion to Buddha and for the benefit of all sentient beings.

MAKING PROSTRATIONS TO THE BUDDHAS

It is good to do a certain number of prostrations (say, 108) each day. With each prostration the name of a buddha should be repeated and, if this name can be repeated many times, that is the best purification indeed since it is reciting the actual name that brings purification. As a prostration is made, a person sees themselves prostrating in all their past lives, and that all sentient beings are prostrating with them. Then, as your head touches the ground, say the next buddha's name.

Just saying Guru Shakyamuni's holy name one time has the power to purify the negative karmas accumulated in 40,000 eons. The same thing happens with the rest of the buddhas. There is a buddha who especially purifies the negative karma of killing; another who purifies the negative karma of stealing; a buddha who purifies the five uninterrupted negative karmas; and so on. The very last of the thirty-five buddhas has the power to purify the heavy negative karmas accumulated in the relationship with a guru, such as criticizing the guru or uttering a heresy. So each buddha has a particular function. Repeating each buddha's name just once has the power to purify negative karmas accumulated in one eon, four eons, 10,000 eons, or 40,000 eons and so on. If the name is repeated more than once, the number of eons is multiplied.

It is emphasized in all the lineages of the Lam-Rim (graduated path to enlightenment) that there is no better method than prostration to purify negative karma and accumulate merit. When one prostration is made, however many atoms of the person's body touches the ground accumulates to be reborn 1,000 times as the universal king. Why is the universal king so important? He is the one who controls the four continents of the mandala, and to be reborn as such requires infinite merit.

In the sutra teachings it is also said that accumulating merit is gradual. If you pull the bridle this way, the horse goes this way; if you pull the bridle the other way, the horse goes the other way. So your direction is in your own hands, depending on how and where you dedicate the merits. If all the merits accumulated by making prostrations are dedicated to receiving enlightenment, making prostrations therefore becomes the cause of this. That is one of the reasons why it has such incredible benefits.

One very highly realized lama of the Lam-Rim lineage asked his guru, "What is the most powerful virtuous action that one should practice to purify negative karmas?" And his guru advised him, "There is no other method more powerful than prostrations by repeating the thirty-five buddhas' names." Then this Lam-Rim-lineage lama, even though he was over eighty-five, was making three hundred prostrations every day. There are many stories like this of lamas who have actualized the Lam-Rim.

AS TOLD BY ONE OF THE GURUS OF LAMA TSONGKHAPA
(1357–1419)

THE FULL PROSTRATION TO THE
THIRTY-FIVE CONFESSION BUDDHAS

When one has become familiar with the buddhas, the following mantra is chanted three times with a prostration for each:

OM NAMO MANJUSHRIYE
NAMA SUSHRIYE, NAMA UTTAMA
SHRIYE SVAHA

I (NAME OF PERSON), THROUGHOUT ALL TIMES;
  I TAKE REFUGE IN THE GURU;
I TAKE REFUGE IN THE BUDDHA;
I TAKE REFUGE IN THE DHARMA;
I TAKE REFUGE IN THE SANGHA.

Three prostrations are then made to each buddha,
and the buddha's name is recited— making a total of 108
prostrations (including the three accompanying the mantra,
as described above). If a person cannot do the prostrations
because they are physically unable, then saying the names of
the buddhas aloud while putting the hands together in the
prostration mudra is the most important thing and will purify and
accumulate merit. Following the prostrations, the prayer to the
thirty-five Confession buddhas is then recited.

THE PRAYER TO THE THIRTY-FIVE
CONFESSION BUDDHAS

The Vajra family of Akshobhya (blue):

1. To the Founder, Bhagavan, Tathagata, arhat, perfectly completed
    Buddha, glorious conqueror Shakyamuni Buddha, I prostrate.
2. To Tathagata, Thoroughly Destroying with Vajra Essence, I prostrate
3. To Tathagata, Radiant Jewel, I prostrate
4. To Tathagata, Lord of the Nagas [snakes], I prostrate
5. To Tathagata, Army of Heroes, I prostrate
6. To Tathagata, Delighted Hero, I prostrate
7. To Tathagata, Jewel Fire, I prostrate

The Tathagata family of Vairochana (white):

8. To Tathagata, Jewel Moonlight, I prostrate
9. To Tathagata, Meaningful to see, I prostrate
10. To Tathagata, Jewel Moon, I prostrate
11. To Tathagata, Stainless One, I prostrate
12. To Tathagata, Bestowed with Courage, I prostrate
13. To Tathagata, Pure One, I prostrate
14. To Tathagata, Bestowed with Purity, I prostrate

The Ratna family of Ratnasambhava (yellow):

15. To Tathagata, Water God, I prostrate
16. To Tathagata, Deity of the Water God, I prostrate
17. To Tathagata, Glorious Goodness, I prostrate
18. To Tathagata, Glorious Sandalwood, I prostrate
19. To Tathagata, Infinite Splendor, I prostrate
20. To Tathagata, Glorious Light, I prostrate
21. To Tathagata, Sorrowless Glory, I prostrate

The Lotus family of Amitabha (red):

22. To Tathagata, Son of Non-craving, I prostrate
23. To Tathagata, Glorious Flower, I prostrate
24. To Tathagata, Pure Light Rays Clearly Knowing by Play, I prostrate
25. To Tathagata, Lotus Light Rays Clearly Knowing by Play, I prostrate
26. To Tathagata, the Glorious Wealth, I prostrate
27. To Tathagata, Glorious Mindfulness, I prostrate
28. To Tathagata, Glorious Name Widely Renowned, I prostrate

The Karma family of Amoghasiddhi (green):

29. To Tathagata, King Holding the Victory Banner of Foremost Power, I prostrate
30. To Tathagata, Glorious One Totally Subduing, I prostrate
31. To Tathagata, Utterly Victorious in Battle, I prostrate
32. To Tathagata, Glorious Transcendence Through Subduing, I prostrate
33. To Tathagata, Glorious Manifestations Illuminating All, I prostrate
34. To Tathagata, All-subduing Jewel Lotus, I prostrate
35. To Tathagata, arhat, perfectly completed buddha, King of the Lord of Mountains, Firmly Seated on Jewel and Lotus, I prostrate.

THE CONFESSION TO THE THIRTY-FIVE BUDDHAS

All you thirty-five buddhas, and those thus gone, tathagatas, arhats, perfectly completed buddhas who are existing, sustaining, and residing in all the world systems of the ten directions. All you buddhas, please give me your attention.

In this life, and throughout beginningless lives in all the realms of samsara, I have created, caused others to create, and rejoiced at the creation of negative karmas, such as misusing offerings to holy objects, misusing offerings to the Sangha, stealing the possessions of the Sangha of the ten directions; I have caused others to create these negative actions and rejoiced at their creation.

I have created the five heinous actions, caused others to create them and rejoiced at their creation.

I have committed the ten non-virtuous actions, involved others in them, and rejoiced at their involvement.

Being obscured by all this karma, I have created the cause for myself and other sentient beings to be reborn in the hells, as animals, as pretas (those living in one of the lower realms of existence), in irreligious places, among barbarians, as long-lived gods, with imperfect senses, holding wrong views, and being displeased with the presence of a buddha.

Now before these buddhas, transcendent destroyers who have become transcendental wisdom, who have become the compassionate eye, who have become witnesses, who have become valid and see with their omniscient minds, I am confessing and accepting all these actions as negative. I will not conceal or hide them, and from now on I will refrain from committing these negative actions.

Buddhas and transcendent destroyers, please give me your attention. In this life and throughout beginningless lives in all the realms of samsara, whatever root of virtue I have created through even the smallest acts of charity, such as giving one mouthful of food to a being born as an animal; whatever root of virtue I have created by abiding in pure conduct; whatever root of virtue I have created by fully ripening sentient beings' minds; whatever root of virtue I have created by generating bodhichitta; whatever root of virtue I have created of the highest transcendent wisdom.

Bringing together all these merits, of both myself and others, I now dedicate them to the highest of which there is no higher, to that even above the highest, to the highest of the high. Thus I dedicate them completely to the highest, fully accomplished enlightenment.

Just as the buddhas and transcendent destroyers of the past have dedicated, just as the buddhas and transcendent destroyers of the future will dedicate, and just as the buddhas and transcendent destroyers of the present are dedicating, in the same way I make this dedication.

I confess all my negative actions separately and rejoice in all merits. I implore the buddhas to grant my request, that I may realize the ultimate, sublime, highest transcendental wisdom.
To the sublime kings of the human beings living now, to those of the past, and to those who have yet to appear, to all those whose knowledge is as vast as the infinite ocean, with my hands folded in respect, I go for refuge.

4

It is compassion that helps us to perfect

our wisdom and our power ...

The transformed mind is ultimate healing.

Meeting the
Medicine Buddha

THE MEDICINE BUDDHA' S HOLY MANTRA

TADYATHA OM BEKHANDZYE BEKHANDZYE MAHA
BEKHANDZYE RADZA SAMUDGATE SVAHA.

he following is recited, then the mantra:

Bhagavan, with equal compassion for all. Whose name when just
heard dispels lower realms suffering. Dispeller of disease and the
three poisons (ignorance, hatred, and attachment), I prostrate to
the Medicine Buddha Lapis Light.

Tadyatha means "like this."

Om is composed of the three pure sounds that signify the holy body, speech, and mind.

Bekhandzye means "eliminating pain." What eliminates pain is medicine. But this is not ordinary pain: the first elimination is the pain of true suffering, the second is the true cause of suffering. The medicine is to take two paths that are part of the path to enlightenment.

Maha Bekhandzye means " great eliminating pain" and refers to the graduated path of the higher capable being, which eliminates the subtle defilements. So Bekhandzye Bekhandzye Maha Bekhandzye contains the whole path to enlightenment: the ultimate medicine.

Radza means "king."

Samudgate means "he who has come forth."

Svaha means establishing a foundation in the heart: the blessing, the devotion from which the realization comes.

So the Medicine Buddha mantra implies that, by actualizing the path contained in Bekhandzye Bekhandzye Maha Bekhandzye – the whole Lam-Rim, or graduated path to enlightenment – a person is able to cease all defilements (both gross and subtle) and purify and transform the ordinary body, speech, and mind into the vajra holy body, speech, and mind. After this, one is able to do perfect work for other sentient beings.

The Medicine Buddha is the
color of lapis lazuli. He holds
a nectar bowl as a symbol of
his healing power. Around
the border of this thangka
painting his mantra is
inscribed in Tibetan.

Medicine of a divine kind

When I first met the Medicine Buddha, I was mesmerized by the brilliance of the deep, translucent lapis blue that colors his face and body. The Medicine Buddha is a powerful cosmic buddha who manifests the healing essence of all enlightened beings. Meditating fervently on this buddha, with a mind made pure by faith and devotion, is acknowledged by followers of the Buddhist path to be the best way to cure disease.

Such meditation is medicine of a divine kind, the sort of cure where the side-effects – a heightened sense of peace and tranquility; a feeling of real healing that engages the body, mind, and spirit – are a bonus. There simply is no greater or better cure. The Medicine Buddha allows the samsaric patient to transcend pain and, sometimes, the creeping realization of approaching death. But it is a realization accompanied by calm acceptance. Death may be near, but you know there is nothing to fear, for the Buddha is there to guide you through the intermediate stage prior to the next rebirth.

My guru, Lama Kyabje Zopa Rinpoche, often urges me to meditate on the seven images of the Medicine buddhas. When I said to him, "But why, Rinpoche, for I am not sick?" he gave me one of his gentle smiles. "The Medicine Buddha is good for everyone, everything," he said. So I followed Rinpoche's advice and filled my home with beautiful thangkas of the blue buddha's presence. For a whole year I was mesmerized by his hypnotic gaze and beautiful body each time I entered my home, for I had the most gorgeous Medicine Buddha thangka displayed facing my entrance door. The Chinese have always believed that if you have an altar where you make offerings to the Buddha, it is auspicious to place it directly facing the main door. So my Medicine Buddha dominated the foyer of my home, and nothing made me feel better.

The Medicine Buddha brings enormous happiness – a feeling that is contagious – so when you meditate on his deep-blue image you are soon surrounded by a pervasive sense of joy, fearlessness, and deepening contentment.

I loved the thangka so much that I commissioned a second one, this time instructing the painters to put more gold in the halo surrounding the Buddha. I intended it to be an offering to Rinpoche when I saw him in Singapore on Wesak day (the festival in May that celebrates the birth, enlightenment, and death of the Buddha). I expected him to be extremely pleased because, being an accomplished artist himself, he loves beautiful religious art (thangkas especially). So I was disappointed that all I got in acknowledgment of my gift was a cursory nod. At least, that was how I perceived his response. It was something of a restraint on my enthusiasm.

Those were early days, of course, when giving a gift to the lama was something of a performance for me. Rinpoche was very skilful in teaching me the huge importance of developing non-attachment: to objects, to people, and even to outcomes. So I should have known that, no matter how much he liked something, he would never go overboard about it. It was an abject lesson in equanimity – something I have always needed. Later I was told that the more Rinpoche likes something, the less fuss he makes about it. This is his way of guarding against rising feelings of attachment. But my fragile ego was to receive another blow, for worse was to come.

The day after I gave the painting to Rinpoche he promptly gave it away to a lady who came to see him. Even as I write this, I am appalled by my delusions and by the strong attachment that I have to the concept of "face." I felt that Rinpoche was really not giving me what was due to me. But "face," or worth, is of course nothing more than the ego!

So the giving away of my precious gift came as a huge slap in the face to me. I heard about it through someone else and was barely able to hide the flush of red creeping up my cheeks. Seeing my shock, Roger Kunsang, Rinpoche's private secretary, said to me, "You can rejoice, Lillian, that you made it possible for Rinpoche to have a suitable gift for the lady. She has done a lot to help the meditation center here, and Rinpoche wanted to demonstrate his gratitude, so your thangka came in extremely useful indeed." Mentally transformed by this comment, I immediately felt better. Roger then told me about something that happened a few days earlier.

A very devoted student had presented Lama Kyabje Zopa Rinpoche with a solid-gold Rolex watch. Rinpoche was very happy indeed and thanked the student profusely for such a beautiful gift, but explained that he would have little use for such an expensive watch. Nevertheless, the student insisted that Rinpoche should keep it. After receiving blessings, he made way for the next person, for of course there is always a queue of people waiting to see Rinpoche.

The next student made three prostrations and then went up to Rinpoche for his blessing. As he came nearer, the guru showed him the gold Rolex and together they admired the beautiful watch. Then, to the amazement of the student, Rinpoche presented him with it. When this second student went out to the others who were waiting to see Rinpoche, he could barely contain his excitement and showed everyone the beautiful gift that the lama had given him – a solid gold Rolex!

The man who had originally given the gift was still around. He was made speechless by Rinpoche's skilful teaching on non-attachment. Like me, he had shock written all over his face. Such is the consummate skill of our guru.

My precious guru, Lama Kyabje Zopa Rinpoche, and me in Singapore.

A Buddha statue towers over a tiny Kathmandu
park, symbolizing the ever-present healing
power of the Buddha.

The image of the Medicine Buddha

The Medicine Buddha looks very similar to Shakyamuni Buddha, but with two essential differences. The first concerns their body color, for the body of Shakyamuni is golden, while that of the Medicine Buddha is bright, lapis blue. The second lies in the hand mudra. Shakyamuni's right hand is in the touching-the-earth gesture, while the Medicine Buddha's right hand is in the mudra of giving, with the palm facing outward so that the sign of the wheel is visible on his inner palm. Both buddhas hold a bowl in the left hand, but while Shakyamuni's bowl is traditionally a begging bowl, that of the Medicine Buddha contains the nectar of cures and healing herbs.

The Medicine Buddha is said to be so powerful that anyone just hearing his name – Bhaishajyaguru – and reciting his mantra will never be reborn in the lower realms! This particular advice was transmitted by none other than Shakyamuni Buddha himself and was recorded by his attendant, Ananda. Buddha went on to say that "even the animals who hear the Medicine Buddha's name will never get reborn in the hell realms" – and this is true whether or not they have faith in the Buddha. I am convinced that my dogs and fish at home will gain human rebirths, because for twenty-four hours a day they can look into the serene gaze of the Medicine Buddha from their basket, pond, and aquarium.

So when someone whom we love is dying, the best thing we can do is recite the names of the seven Medicine Buddhas loudly in the ear of the dying person; or recite the Medicine Buddha mantra into a cassette and then play that continually. Even patients in a coma can respond to the sound of this magical mantra. Simply by doing this you might well save the person in question from the suffering of the lower realms for many eons, for you will have ensured the care of the Buddha, should that person succumb and pass on to the next life.

The Medicine Buddha's right hand is in the mudra of giving, or Varada mudra. His left hand is in the meditation mudra and holds a nectar-filled bowl.

The Medicine Buddha's blessings are cosmic, transcending all lifetimes – past, present, and future. When you faithfully perform his meditation, not only will you be cured of all the ailments of this life, but of future lives as well. And you will gain precious human rebirth once more, thereby enabling you to continue with your Dharma practice and progress on your spiritual journey.

The source of the Medicine Buddha's power of healing, and his power of saving beings from the hell realm, is his unsurpassed compassion for all sentient beings. The story goes that in the past, when the Medicine Buddha was a bodhisattva (someone who has realized the desire to attain enlightenment for the sake of all beings, but has not yet become a Buddha), he made many prayers and dedications with intense compassion that his name alone should be wish-fulfilling and should bring happiness, so that when he became enlightened all heartfelt prayers addressed to the Medicine Buddha would get answered. Merely chanting his name thus becomes a cause of enlightenment – such an unbelievably easy way to liberate ourselves and help others.

Benefits of the Medicine Buddha practice

Many benefits arise from doing the Medicine Buddha practice or merely from reciting his holy mantra. For example, by reciting the mantra over a medicine, its power can be increased.

The medicine is placed in a bowl in front of the person doing the practice, and they visualize a moon disk above it. Standing on the moon disk is a blue OM, surrounded by the syllables of the Medicine Buddha mantra – Tadayatha Om Bekhandzye Maha Bekhandzye Radza Samudgate Svaha – running in a clockwise direction. The mantra is recited and nectar is visualized, flowing down from the syllables of the mantra and being absorbed into the medicine. The syllables and the moon then dissolve into the medicine, which now becomes very powerful, possessing both medical and spiritual cures. When treating someone with cancer, for example, the practitioner imagines that the medicine has the specific power to cure it. The more faith a person possesses and the more mantras they recite, the more powerful the medicine will be.

Tibetan doctors use Medicine Buddha meditation and mantras to bless the remedies they prepare. They believe that the medicine is then more effective. In addition to the power of the medicinal plants and other substances that it contains, its spiritual power will help bring about a purification of the mind, thereby causing a speedy recovery.

For healers, it is valuable to do a Medicine Buddha retreat for a month or two, and to recite his name and mantra every day. If this is practiced, it is said that the medicinal goddesses and protectors will help a healer to make correct diagnoses of patients' illnesses and prescribe the right treatments. By practicing these methods, clairvoyance may be gained. A sign of attainment is that, before patients come to a healer in person, they visit the healer in their dreams, and the healer diagnoses their illness; the next day they come to see the healer in person, who can then prescribe the exact treatment they need. Another sign is that when a healer concentrates on a patient's pulse, they can immediately recognize the disease and prescribe the right remedy. As the healer focuses on the pulse, goddesses may also appear in space around them, and tell them the nature of the disease and its treatment.

SOLVING ANY PROBLEM

Medicine Buddha practice also purifies broken vows, such as the Pratimoksha vows, or precepts, taken by Buddhists as part of their Dharma practice. Rinpoche says that the Medicine Buddha is also very powerful for purifying negative karma and gaining many different kinds of success. According to the Medicine Buddha sutra, we can actually use his puja for any purpose, any problem: to resolve court cases, stop wars, prevent violence; it is also very good for business, and in enabling women who are pregnant to give birth successfully. Finally, it is useful for the most important success of all: to gain the realizations of the Lam-Rim, the graduated path to enlightenment. These kinds of success will enable you to make your life beneficial to all beings and, ultimately, to attain enlightenment.

Rinpoche once referred to the writings of the Fifth Dalai Lama, as well as the biographies of the lineage lamas. He read how they were able to benefit many beings, practice the teachings of Buddha, and receive great realizations – all by doing the Medicine Buddha practice. Rinpoche told us that the great Dharma king of Tibet, Lha Lama Yeshe Oe, who invited the incomparable Lama Atisha to Tibet, did the Medicine Buddha practice on every eighth day of the Tibetan month (the same as Tara day) and on the fifteen special days of the Buddha performing miracles (the first fifteen days of the first Tibetan month). The king was eventually captured and put in prison near Nepal, where he passed away. When they cremated his holy body, rainbow lights emitted from the fire and there were rainfalls of flowers for seven days. Then a Medicine Buddha, the size of a thumb, appeared from his heart, the sky was filled with music, and there were many wonderful signs. All of the lineage lamas of the Medicine Buddha who did puja on the eighth day of every lunar month also had incredible realizations. And when they passed away there were wonderful signs, similar to those that appeared for King Lha Lama Yeshe Oe.

Monks performing a Medicine Buddha puja at Kopan monastery, Nepal.

BENEFITING ANIMALS AND INSECTS

When eating meat, the Medicine Buddha mantra can be recited (see page 92) and the meat blown over to purify instantly the animal's negative karma. No matter how far away its consciousness may be, it receives the blessing effect of the mantra, which then helps it to a higher rebirth. House insects, such as ants, mosquitoes, bugs, and so on, can have their negative karmas purified, which helps them to experience a good rebirth; the mantra is recited, and the insects are blown upon. This fulfils the purpose of them coming into a house. It makes their lives meaningful and, because we can benefit them in this way, it makes human life meaningful, too.

Some years ago Rinpoche lead a retreat in Big Sur in the United States, in a cabin near the water. Many ants used to come into the kitchen, so he sent three tsa-tsas of the Medicine Buddha (small bas-relief images) to the cooks and told them that each time they found ants or insects in the house they should put them in a plastic bag, without sealing the container, then hold a tsa-tsa in one hand and with the other hand turn the bag clockwise at the same level. With each turn, all of the ants created the cause for enlightenment and for liberation from samsara; they also created the cause for happiness in their future lives for hundreds of thousands of lifetimes. Rinpoche explained that this was such an easy way to practice the Dharma, to liberate the ants, and cause them to have a good rebirth.

Since hearing that story, I have had a really hard time handling the insects that come into my home, because implied in Rinpoche's story was an unspoken behest not kill such creatures! However, with determined practice in accordance with Rinpoche's advice, I have discovered that I no longer look on them as pests. Each time such creatures come, I have trained my staff not to kill them with insecticide or chemical poison; instead, we now try to take them around the holy objects in my home – paintings of buddhas, altars, prayer wheels, and stupas – at least three times in a clockwise direction.

This way, simply by coming into my house, these creatures give me the chance to perform the best Dharma practice – helping beings who really cannot, or do not know how to, help themselves. Hopefully, by taking them round my stupa and reciting mantras on their behalf, I have planted the seeds of liberation in their consciousness.

As a follow-up to these practices, one day a beautiful bird flew into my garden, landing directly at my feet. He looked at me with wide eyes, neither fearful nor excited. Immediately, for no reason at all, I cupped him in my hands and ran inside to circumambulate my stupa three times, which has statues of many buddhas. Then I took the bird to gaze at the Medicine Buddha, reciting the mantra silently on his behalf. I took him outside again to look for a safe place for him to rest. As soon as I placed him on the ground, the bird jerked his head and died. Amazingly, he seems to have come to me, I think, to allow me to create the cause for him to gain a human rebirth – what fantastic karma!

Buddhists treat animals with care and respect. They also practice animal liberation rituals in which captive animals due to be killed are released into their natural habitat and so have their lives extended. This is one of the most powerful ways of attaining longevity. By saving the lives of creatures and extending their life span, one creates the cause for living longer as humans – and this truly is vital, because as long as we are alive we are able to do practices that will help propel us into a good rebirth.

The Medicine Buddha and Tibetan medicine

The full name of the Medicine Buddha is Bhaishajyaguru Vaiduryaprabha, the Healing Master of Lapis Lazuli Radiance. Like Shakyamuni, he wears the robes of a monk and is seated in the full cross-legged posture. His left hand is in the meditation mudra, resting in his lap and holding a bowl filled with medicinal nectar. His right hand rests on his knee, with the palm facing outward in the mudra of granting blessings; it holds the stem of a myrobalan plant (Terminalia chebula), which is renowned as the king among medicines because of its effectiveness in treating both mental and physical diseases.

In traditional Tibetan thangkas, the Lapis Healing Master is shown in a group of either seven or eight Medicine buddhas, one of whom is Shakyamuni Buddha himself. In paintings that show the Medicine Buddha in his eastern Pure Land, known as Pure Lapis Lazuli, the Healing Master is flanked by two bodhisattvas of that land, Suryaprabha and Chandraprabha, known respectively as "All-Pervading Solar Radiance" and "All-Pervading Lunar Radiance."

The deep blue of the Medicine Buddha is that of lapis lazuli, a precious stone greatly prized by Asian and European cultures for more than 6,000 years. An aura of mystery surrounds this gemstone. It is mined principally in the remote Badakhshan region of northeast Afghanistan, an almost inaccessible area in Central Asia. One commentator has written, "The finest specimens of lapis, intensely blue with speckled waves and swirls of shining gold-colored pyrite, resemble the night aglow with myriads of stars." Traditionally this beautiful stone was used to symbolize that which is pure or rare. It is said to have a curative or strengthening effect upon those who wear it, and its deep blue light has demonstrable healing powers on those who use it in visualization practices. Its natural smoothness allows it to be polished to a high degree of reflectivity.

The Medicine Buddha is one of the most popular buddhas in the Buddhist pantheon. The sutras describe his eastern Pure Land with the same reverence that is reserved for Sukhavati, the western paradise of Amitabha. Rebirth in this land of lapis lazuli is said to be as conducive to enlightenment as rebirth in the western paradise. Reciting the Medicine Buddha mantra, or merely voicing his holy name, is sufficient to grant release from the lower realms, protection from worldly dangers, and freedom from untimely death.

In Tibet, the Medicine Buddha is revered as the source of the healing arts, and it is through him that the teachings embodied in the Four Medical Tantras, the basis of Tibetan medicine, came into being. According to the first of these Tantras, the Lapis Lazuli Medicine Buddha was once seated in meditation and surrounded by an assembly of disciples, who included divine physicians, great sages, non-Buddhist gods, and bodhisattvas – all of whom wished to learn the art of healing. However, seated in front of the radiance that poured forth from the Buddha, they were rendered speechless and so were unable to request the desired teachings. But the Buddha was in tune with their unspoken wishes and thus manifested two emanation beings, one to request the teachings and the other to deliver them. In this way, detailed teachings on various mental and physical ailments, their causes, diagnoses, and treatment, and the maintenance of health, were said to have originated from the great Buddha of healing.

If these sentient beings those plunged into the depths of samsara suffering hear the name of the Lord Master of Healing, the Lapis Lazuli Radiance Tathagata, and with the utmost sincerity accept it and hold on to it, and no doubts arise, then they will not fall into a woesome path.

BUDDHA SHAKYAMUNI'S WORDS TO HIS DISCIPLE
AND ATTENDANT, ANANDA.

The root of all diseases

In accordance with the Four Medical Tantras, every disease originates from the three poisonous delusions: ignorance, hatred, and attachment. These three delusions lead to imbalances in the three bodily humors (phlegm, wind, and bile), in the various bodily constituents (blood, flesh, bone, and so on) and in waste products or impurities (excrement, urine, and perspiration). All of these are analyzed into twenty-five divisions.

If all twenty-five areas are in balance and the three factors of the tastes, the inherent qualities of your food, and your behavior are wholesome, then your health and life will flourish. If they are not in balance, then your health and life will be harmed, and that imbalance will spread over the skin, increase in the flesh, move along the vessels, meet the bones, and descend into the solid and hollow organs.

Treatment of disease and the maintenance of health are required to bring the various elements of the body back into balance. There are four progressive treatments for this. The first two require changes in approach – that is, in the type of food we eat and in our behavior. Only when these prove ineffective is the physician advised to prescribe medicine. And only when this also fails is he or she to resort to external forms of treatment, such as cauterization. However, none of the treatments has a lasting effect unless it is accompanied by spiritual transformation.

If ignorance and associated delusions remain festering within us, sooner or later they give rise to disease and the recurring misery of cyclic existence. Buddhas such as Shakyamuni and the Medicine Buddha are revered as great physicians not because of their healing powers – great though these are – but because they have the compassion, wisdom, and skilful means to diagnose and treat the root delusions that underlie all mental and physical afflictions.

The Medicine Buddha sadhana

To practice the Medicine Buddha sadhana, the best way is to seek the advice of a qualified lama. Even better, request and receive initiation, or at least oral transmission of the mantra (which is like getting permission to practice it). Because initiation and oral transmission is handed down in an unbroken lineage, it carries the blessings of the Buddha himself and of all the highly qualified lamas right down to the guru, from whom the transmission is received. It is powerful stuff, so the practice should be approached with pure motivation – the genuine desire to generate a good heart and attain enlightenment.

Remember that when meditating and reciting mantras to the Medicine Buddha, the healing power really originates from the thought of loving kindness, compassion, and bodhichitta. Motivation is the key to the power of prayers. Visualizing the Buddha image and reciting mantras enhances the healing power of the practice, but these are techniques to turn motivation into reality. So the motivation itself is vital.

Lama Kyabje Zopa Rinpoche's advice to those who have recovered from serious illness is not only to do meditation practices and recite mantras, but to generate a positive, altruistic motivation. Still, it seems that some people have recovered from cancer simply by visualizing a white light and having strong faith in the healing Buddha. Sometimes people have recovered by doing meditation practices themselves and at other times by having someone else do the practices for them. Rinpoche says it is better if the sick person does the meditation, since the healing takes longer when someone else does it; when both do it, this helps.

Overleaf is a summarized sadhana and visualization, which Lama Kyabje Zopa Rinpoche translated and composed for his students around the world. For the full sadhana text, contact the FPMT (Foundation for the Preservation of the Mahayana Tradition), which offers this and other meditation sadhanas as free downloads from its websites, or at a small cost from its Education Office (see pages 263–268).

INTRODUCTION TO THE MEDICINE BUDDHA VISUALIZATION

When this Medicine Buddha practice is performed for a sick or dying person or an animal, the seven Medicine Buddhas are visualized, one above another, stacked above him or her. First, the nectar is visualized, flowing from the Medicine Buddha at the very top, Renowned Glorious King of Excellent Signs, purifying the beings of all their negative karma and obscuration. The name of the Renowned Glorious King of Excellent Signs is recited seven times, then this is absorbed into the Medicine buddha below. In the same way, visualizing nectars flowing down from the topmost Medicine buddha, the name of each Medicine buddha is recited seven times, then they are allowed to be absorbed into the buddha below. With the final Medicine buddha, many mantras may be recited, and again strong nectar purification is visualized. The person imagines that the person or animal has been completely purified, that no negative karma exists in their consciousness. Their body has become as calm and as clear as crystal.

The Medicine Buddha then melts into light, absorbed into the person or animal, thereby blessing their body, speech, and mind, which becomes one with the Medicine Buddha's holy body, holy speech, and holy mind. The practitioner meditates strongly on this oneness.

He or she then thinks of light beams flowing from the Medicine buddhas to purify all other sentient beings, especially those who are sick with disease. Or, the Medicine buddhas are visualized above the crown of each sentient being's head, thereby purifying them. Particular focus is given to the person or animal being prayed for; also, seven Medicine buddhas are visualized above the crown of every other sentient being's head.

In Medicine Buddha visualizations, the Medicine Buddha radiates beams of white light that purify and heal sickness in the world.

THE PRACTICE

Pure motivation is generated by thinking the following:

The purpose of my life is not just to solve my own problems and find happiness for myself, but to free every living being from all their suffering and bring them to the peerless happiness of full enlightenment. For this reason I need to develop my mind, to develop my wisdom and compassion. By actualizing this path of mental healing, I free my mind from all gross and subtle obscurations. To succeed in this I need to have a long life and be free from outer obstacles, such as disease, and from inner obstacles, negative thoughts, and actions and their imprints on my mind. Therefore, to benefit and bring happiness to every living being, I am doing this meditation on the Medicine buddhas.

VISUALIZATIONS AND MEDITATIONS

A lotus flower is visualized four inches (ten centimeters) above the crown of the head. In the center of the lotus is a white moon disk on which is seated the root guru, in the form of the Medicine Buddha. He is blue in color, and his body radiates a blue light. His right hand is in the mudra of granting sublime realization, resting on his right knee and holding the stem of a myrobalan plant between his thumb and index finger. His left hand, in the mudra of concentration, holds a lapis-lazuli bowl filled with healing nectar. Seated in the vajra position, he is wearing the three robes of a monk. He has all the signs and qualities of a buddha.

    The person doing the visualization takes refuge in the Medicine Buddha and generates bodhichitta, reflecting three times on this meditation:

I go for refuge until I am enlightened, to the Buddha, Dharma, and Sangha – the spiritual community. By the virtuous merits I amass by practicing compassion and other perfections, may I quickly attain buddhahood so that I may lead all sentient beings into enlightenment.

The Four Immeasurable Thoughts are generated. This meditation is reflected upon three times:

1. May all beings abide in equanimity, free of attachment and hatred, not holding some close and others distant. I will cause them to abide in equanimity. Please, Guru Buddha, grant me blessings to do this.

2. May all beings have happiness and the causes of happiness. I will bring them happiness and its causes. Please, Guru Buddha, grant me blessings to do this.

3. May all beings be free from suffering and the causes of suffering. I will free them from suffering and its causes. Please, Guru Buddha, grant me blessings to do this.

4. May all beings never be separated from the happiness of higher rebirth and liberation. I will cause them never to be separated from this happiness. Please, Guru Buddha, grant me blessings to do this.

Special bodhichitta is then cultivated. This meditation is contemplated:

Especially for the benefit of all mother sentient beings, I will quickly, very quickly, attain the precious state of perfect and complete buddhahood. For this reason I will practice this yoga method of Guru Medicine Buddha.

THE SEVEN-LIMBED PRAYER

The seven-limbed prayer is recited in the mind or aloud:
Reverently I prostrate with my body, speech, and mind
And present clouds of every type of offering, actual and imagined,
I confess all negative actions accumulated during beginningless time,
And I rejoice in the virtues of all holy and ordinary beings.
Please remain until samsara ends,
And turn the wheel of Dharma for all sentient beings.
I dedicate all the virtues of myself and others to the great enlightenment.

A mandala offering is made (either this one or the long mandala offering, see
page 256). The following is strongly visualized:

This ground, anointed with perfume, strewn with flowers,
Adorned with Mount Meru, four continents, the sun and the moon:
I imagine this as a buddha-field and offer it.
May all living beings enjoy this Pure Land.
IDAM GURU RATNA MANDALAKAM NIRYATAYAMI.

SUPPLICATION TO THE MEDICINE BUDDHA

The following supplication to the Medicine Buddha is recited:

- I beseech you, Bhagawan Medicine Buddha, whose sky-colored holy body of lapis lazuli signifies omniscient wisdom and compassion as vast as limitless space, please grant me your blessings.
- I beseech you, Guru Medicine Buddha, Compassionate One, who holds in your right hand the king of medicines, symbolizing your vow to help the pitiful migratory beings afflicted by the 424 diseases, please grant me your blessings.
- I beseech you, Guru Medicine Buddha, Compassionate One, who holds in your left hand a bowl of nectar, symbolizing your vow to give the glorious immortal nectar of Dharma to eliminate the degenerations of sickness, old age, and death, please grant me your blessings.

THE VISUALIZATION OF THE SEVEN MEDICINE BUDDHAS

The visualization of the seven Medicine buddhas is performed:

Above the crown of Guru Medicine Buddha a wish-granting jewel is visualized, which in essence is one's guru.

Above him, on a lotus and moon disk, is the Buddha Delightful King of Clear Knowing, whose body is red. His right hand is in the mudra of bestowing sublime realizations and his left hand is in the mudra of concentration.

Above him, on a lotus and moon disk, is the Buddha Melodious Ocean of Proclaimed Dharma, whose body is yellow and whose hands are in the same mudras.

Above him, on a lotus and moon disk, is the Buddha Supreme Glory Free from Sorrow, pink in color, with both hands in the mudra of concentration.

Above him, on a lotus and moon disk, is the Buddha Stainless Excellent Gold, pale yellow in color, with his right hand in the mudra of expounding Dharma and his left in the mudra of concentration.

Above him, on a lotus and moon disk, is the Buddha King of Melodious Sound, Brilliant Radiance of Skill Adorned with Jewels, Moon, and Lotus, reddish-yellow in color, with his right hand expounding the Dharma and his left hand in the mudra of concentration.

Above him, on a lotus and moon disk, is the Buddha Renowned Glorious King of Excellent Signs, yellow in color, with his right hand in the mudra of expounding the Dharma and his left hand in the mudra of concentration.

A thangka painting showing the seven medicine buddhas, with three buddhas in wrathful pose below the central buddha.

REQUESTS TO THE MEDICINE BUDDHAS

With the hands placed together in the mudra of prostration, the following verse is recited seven times with the name of each Medicine buddha (starting from the top). The person making the requests takes strong refuge in that specific buddha, to ensure the quick success of their prayers, whether they are praying for someone to recover from an illness or for the success of a business or Dharma project. If the Medicine Buddha practice is being done for someone who is dying or who has died, they keep in their heart the request for his or her rebirth in a Pure Land or an upper realm. After the seventh repetition of each verse, the Medicine Buddha above absorbs into the one below.

The following is recited seven times:

> *To the fully realized destroyer of all defilements who sees the true nature of things, perfect Buddha Renowned Glorious King of Excellent Signs [replace this name with the next buddha down each time], to you I prostrate, make offerings, and go for refuge. Please, may whatever vow you have made in the past ripen upon me and all sentient beings right now. May all my pure prayers succeed immediately.*

The Buddha Renowned Glorious King of Excellent Signs is visualized accepting the request with delight, and sends nectar beams that purify the body and mind of all disease, spirit harm, negative karma, and obscuration. Buddha Renowned Glorious King of Excellent Signs then melts into light and is absorbed into the Buddha King of Melodious Sound below. The same verse is repeated seven times (substituting the name of Buddha King of Melodious Sound) and the recitations are continued until all seven Medicine buddhas have been requested and absorbed.

VISUALIZATION FOR THE LONG MEDICINE BUDDHA MANTRA

Infinite beams of white light are emitted from the heart and holy body of Guru Medicine Buddha. They grant a person's requests, and fill their body from head to toe. The light beams purify all their diseases, obscurations and spirit harm and of their causes – negative karma and delusions. Their body becomes as clear as crystal.

The light pours into them a second and third time, filling their body with great bliss. Then Guru Medicine Buddha melts into white or blue light and is absorbed into them through the crown of their head. Their consciousness is purified, and they become the Medicine Buddha. (Those who have not received a great initiation of Kriya Tantra or Highest Yoga Tantra should visualize the Medicine Buddha melting into light, which is absorbed between their eyebrows, thus blessing their body, speech, and mind.) The Medicine Buddha reappears very small at their heart and the lotus, moon disk, OM, and mantra garland appear at the Medicine Buddha's heart.

At the person's heart now appears a lotus and moon disk. Standing at the center of the moon is the blue seed-syllable OM, surrounded by the syllables of the Medicine Buddha mantra. The following mantra is recited and beams of light are visualized, radiating outward in all directions from the syllables at their heart, filling and illuminating all the sentient beings of the Six Realms (see page 61). Through their great love and great compassion, a person purifies the sentient beings of all diseases and spirit harm and obscurations.

Practicing Medicine Buddha sadhanas means creating the motivation to heal all sentient beings.

THE MEDICINE BUDDHA'S LONG MANTRA

OM NAMO BHAGAWATE BEKHANDZYE
GURU BEDURYA PRABHA RADZAYA
TATAGATAYA
ARHATE SAMYAKSAM BUDDHAYA
TADYATHA
OM BEKANDZE BEKHANDZYE
MAHA BEKHANDZYE RADZA
SAMUDGATE SVAHA

At the end of the recitation, it is visualized that all sentient beings are transformed into the aspect of the Medicine Buddha. The person performing the visualization feels a great sense of joy that they have been able to lead sentient beings to this enlightenment.

In a more simplified practice, Guru Medicine Buddha is visualized above the crown of the head and the following is repeated seven times:

To the fully realized destroyer of all defilements who sees the true nature of things, perfect Buddha Medicine Guru, King of Lapis Light, I prostrate, make offerings, and go for refuge. May all the prayers you made in the past and the prayers I am making now be actualized immediately for me and for all other sentient beings.

The mantra is recited, and purifying beams of light are visualized, emitting from the heart and holy body of Guru Medicine Buddha. Sicknesses and spirit harm, as well as their causes, negative karma, and obscurations are eliminated. Then the person doing the visualization imagines that their body is filled with light, and becomes as clear as crystal. The beams radiate out in all directions to heal the sicknesses and afflictions of all other sentient beings.

After the recitation, Guru Medicine Buddha melts into light and is absorbed into the person's heart. Their mind becomes one with the Dharmakaya, the essence of all the buddhas.

DEDICATIONS

Lama Kyabje Zopa Rinpoche always has a very long list of dedications – sometimes longer than the sadhana itself. But none of them is ever made to benefit himself; they are for the benefit of others and all sentient beings.

In my own list of dedications I always include a prayer for the long life of my precious guru. And I pray that everyone who practices what I write about in my books benefits hugely and has eternal happiness.

Here are three excellent dedications:

Due to the merit accumulated from doing this Medicine Buddha practice, may I complete the deeds of the bodhisattvas. May I become the savior, refuge, and guide of all migratory beings, who have been kind to me in numberless past lives.

Due to all my merit in the past, present, and future, may any living being who sees me, hears me, touches me, remembers me, or speaks about me be immediately released from all their suffering and experience perfect happiness for ever.

Due to all the merit I have collected in the three times and all the merit collected by buddhas, bodhisattvas, and other sentient beings, just as the Medicine Buddha's compassion encompasses all beings, may I also become the foundation of the means of living for all sentient beings, who are as extensive as space.

5

A compassionate person is the most powerful
healer, not only of their own disease or problems,
but of those of others.

LAMA KYABJE ZOPA RINPOCHE

Meeting the Compassion Buddha, Avalokiteshvara

AVALOKITESHVARA'S MANTRA

OM MANI PADME HUM

The Compassion Buddha's magical mantra hums across the Universe, bringing solace, comfort, and awakening to those who tune into its holy frequency.

The great Compassion Buddha is the most universally beloved deity of Mahayana Buddhism. Revered by the Chinese as the goddess of mercy, Kuan Yin, and cherished by the Tibetans as their patron, the Compassion Buddha Chenrezig, Avalokiteshvara can be regarded as one of the most visible faces of Buddhism. This enlightened being is universally known to come to the aid of all suffering beings.

In his four-armed form, Avalokiteshvara is the divine protector of Tibet, the Land of Snows, and signifies the all-pervasive blessings of his famous six-syllable mantra, which means "homage to the jewel in the lotus."

His Holiness the Dalai Lama with Lama Kyabje Zopa Rinpoche at Bodhgaya, India, 2001.

The great jewel in the lotus

Avalokiteshvara is the great jewel in the lotus. Manifesting in tender and wrathful forms, he is the embodiment of all the Buddha's infinite compassion. Born from a shaft of clear light emanating from the heart of Buddha Amitabha, which transformed into a lotus, Avalokiteshvara arises in the form of the radiant, white-faced, four-armed Chenrezig so beloved of Tibetan Buddhists. He also manifests with eleven faces and 1,000 hands, reflecting his multi-faceted compassionate work.

Four-armed Chenrezig has one face, four arms, and two legs crossed in the meditation posture. His front two hands are pressed together at his heart, in the mudra of supplication, holding the wish-fulfilling jewel. The jewel signifies Avalokiteshvara's infinite bodhichitta motivation – the intense desire to bring all suffering beings to enlightenment. Of his back two hands, the right one holds the crystal rosary, symbolizing liberation from samsara, while the left holds a blue utpala flower, symbolic of his compassionate motivation, which encompasses the past, present, and future.

The Tibetans believe that His Holiness the Dalai Lama is an emanation of this form of Avalokiteshvara. Indeed, through successive incarnations of the Dalai Lama, Avalokiteshvara's message of compassion has become all-encompassing. Popular myths describe the Tibetan people as being descended from the Compassion Buddha, who in the aspect of a monkey is said to have sired the original peoples of the Land of Snows.

In teachings that I have attended, references have often been made to the monarchs and high lamas of Tibet, who were primarily responsible for propagating the rise of Buddhism there. The king most frequently mentioned is Songtsen Gampo, who lived in the seventh century and is said to have been an emanation of Chenrezig. His two wives (one from China and one from Nepal) are often described as emanations of Tara (see Chapter 7), the female deity universally known as the mother-liberator. Another important figure in the history of Buddhism in Tibet is the eighth-century Guru Rinpoche (also known as Padmasambhava) – the lotus-born guru. He too is said to have been an emanation of the Compassion Buddha.

Avalokiteshvara is also a major presence in many Mahayana sutras that are chanted and read as prayers. He features prominently in the *Heart of the Perfection of Wisdom* sutra, one of the most significant and widely known direct texts from the Buddha, which explains the perfection of wisdom – the understanding of the true nature of existence. It is a universally revered Buddhist text and is recited daily by practicing Buddhists of all traditions. It is said that one reading has the power to purify eons of negative karma. In the Heart Sutra, Avalokiteshvara – in the presence of the Buddha – explains the perfection of wisdom to Sariputra and a gathering of monks and arhats on Vultures Peak Mountain, Raighir, northern India.

JOURNEY TO VULTURE'S PEAK

I have been to Vultures Peak. About a hundred of us – monks and lay people, led by Lama Kyabje Zopa Rinpoche and his wonderful guru, Ribur Rinpoche – embarked on the long, steep climb, and I shall never know how Ribur Rinpoche, who is more than eighty years old, managed it. By the time we reached the top it was dark, chilly, and windy – a contrast to the heat of the ascent. The summit of Vultures Peak is tiny so there was barely enough room for so many of us; so we wedged ourselves between the rocks, taking care not to slip.

By candlelight, Ribur Rinpoche began reading the Heart Sutra in Tibetan – and then from somewhere came a creeping sensation of light. I felt it penetrating my closed eyes as we meditated on the words of Ribur Rinpoche as he read out the sutra in Tibetan. I opened my eyes and, looking up to the skies, saw the clouds slowly separate. From behind them, a bright light was shining, radiating down toward us. It was the most amazing, divine light show and reminded me of a movie I once saw as a child depicting the parting of the Red Sea ... No one else seemed to be looking, and Ribur Rinpoche continued to read. I turned to look at Charok Lama, the ten-year-old reincarnation of another high lama from nearby Lawudo; his eyes were closed in blissful meditation. He, too, seemed oblivious to the rays of light.

I recall taking out my camera and pointing it toward the heavens, so I do have a picture of the sky that holy evening! On film it does not look anything like as awesome as I remember it. But that night, up on Vultures Peak, I really felt the presence of Avalokiteshvara. It was as if he was speaking to us through the speech of Ribur Rinpoche. When later we began the descent – a journey by torchlight – I saw the lamas move alongside us and it seemed to me as though they were gliding – flying down the mountain! For sure, they reached the bottom long before we did.

Much later, when I asked Lama Kyabje Zopa Rinpoche about the bright light in the skies and the speed at which the lamas seemed to move down the mountain, he barely nodded in acknowledgment. They are like that, the high lamas – they rarely dwell on divine happenings. I was left with the feeling such events are something they see and experience all the time.

The story of thousand-armed Chenrezig

The story of Avalokiteshvara's transformation to his thousand-armed form reflects his heartfelt sincerity, which has made him Buddhism's principal icon of compassion.

Before his spiritual father Amitabha, and in the presence of the 1,000 buddhas of this eon, Avalokiteshvara vowed to work unceasingly to end the suffering of all sentient beings. Then, in a moment of intense fervor, he further vowed that, should he ever have the slightest thought of giving up, "May my head be cracked into ten pieces and my body be split into a thousand pieces." Thenceforth Avalokiteshvara entered into a state of prolonged intense and uninterrupted meditation, during which he recited the Om Mani Padme Hum mantra, dedicating the merit to all the beings of the world.

When he finally arose and surveyed everything around him, he noted bitterly that he had succeeded in liberating only a small number of beings from suffering. His heart filled with sorrow, and in frustration he cried out that he was ready to give up. In that instant of despair – true to his vow – his head cracked into ten pieces and his body shattered into 1,000 pieces.

In agony Avalokiteshvara called out to his guru Amitabha, who restored Avalokiteshvara's broken body, transforming it into 1,000 arms, each palm with an all-seeing eye. This increased by 1,000 times the mighty Bodhisattva's capacity to help all sentient beings. In the same way, Amitabha changed the broken head into ten faces, nine of which were fashioned in a compassionate aspect and one in a wrathful aspect. At the top Amitabha placed his own face, indicating how happy he was with Avalokiteshvara's bodhichitta motivation.

This is how Avalokiteshvara came to have the aspect of the eleven-faced, 1,000-armed Chenrezig. This form of the Compassion Buddha is most often depicted in Tibetan thangkas, for it is the form most dearly loved by his Tibetan devotees. Many of the deeply meditative practices are also done in front of this aspect, in particular the retreat purification known as the nyung nay, which comprises fasting and prostrations.

Avalokiteshvara is popularly depicted as the 1,000-armed Chenrezig, with eleven faces and 1,000 arms, each hand having its own radiant, all-seeing eye.

NYUNG NAY AND THE MAHAYANA PRECEPTS

This is a powerful, two-day fasting retreat based on Avalokiteshvara. It is an intensive practice that requires following the eight Mahayana precepts (see overleaf), as well as, on the second day, vows of not eating, drinking, or talking for twenty-four hours. The meditation sessions include the recitation of praises and mantras, as well as making prostrations.

The Mahayana precepts consist of eight vows that one commits to keep for a twenty-four hour period, based on a bodhichitta motivation to achieve enlightenment for all beings. These are the vows not to kill, not to steal, not to engage in sexual activity, and not to tell lies; and there are vows to abstain from alcohol, from using high or expensive beds, from eating food at improper times, from wearing perfume, garlands, or ornaments, from singing and dancing, and so on. It is considered very beneficial to take the eight Mahayana precepts on the auspicious days of the Buddhist calendar, such as days that celebrate Lord Buddha's enlightenment (Wesak day, for example) and the solar or lunar eclipses. On these days taking the precepts multiplies 100,000 times whatever merit is generated.

Reverently I prostrate to holy Avalokiteshvara, who is inseparable from my root guru, who has the thousand arms of the thousand universal monarchs, the thousand eyes of the thousand Buddhas of this good eon, and who manifests whatsoever is appropriate to whomsoever.

In his 1,000-armed form, Avalokiteshvara continues to carry the wish-fulfilling jewel, a crystal rosary, and a uptala flower, but his many other hands are shown holding other auspicious objects, such as a vase, a Dharma wheel, and a bow. Except for the pair in the mudra of supplication at his heart, all the hands are in the mudra of bestowing blessings and realization on all beings. Each palm has an eye to observe the suffering in many worlds. Ten of his faces signify his attainment of the ten bodhisattva stages, as well as helping beings in the ten directions. The eleventh and topmost face of Amitabha signals his universal compassion and the all-encompassing wisdom of the buddhas.

So Avalokiteshvara embodies the compassionate essence of enlightenment raised to its highest power and emanating the boundless love of the great Buddha Amitabha. Since compassion is the one of the twin pillars of Buddhism (the other being wisdom), Avalokiteshvara is himself regarded as one of the pillars of Buddhism.

Young monks performing afternoon prayers and prostrations.

The goddess of mercy, Kuan Yin

I first got to know the Compassion Buddha in the form in which most Chinese know her – as the gentle and graceful Kuan Yin, who is an object of devotion for many millions of Chinese. Her gentle and beautiful form, accompanied by children, dragons, and tortoises, usually shows her holding a fly whisk in one hand and a small vial of holy nectar in the other. Kuan Yin is often shown seated on a lotus, with her hands in the meditation mudra, reminiscent of Amitabha Buddha.

The Chinese have made Avalokiteshvara in her female form, as the goddess of mercy, uniquely their own. Probably due to influences from Tibet in times past, there is also a Chinese 1,000-armed Kuan Yin, just as there is the eleven-faced, 1,000-armed Chenrezig. Kuan Yin personifies, even more than Lord Buddha, the practice of Buddhism among the Chinese, and there are few Buddhist households in Asia that do not have an image of her, for she is the divine being who is turned to most often in times of sadness, grief, and sorrow.

Many Chinese believe that just thinking of Kuan Yin and calling her name causes their burdens to be lightened, their worries to be allayed, and their wounded hearts to heal. The compassion of the goddess of mercy has the power to cause the fire of looming disasters to cease burning instantly; to transform enemies into benefactors; to loosen bonds that imprison; to dissolve all evil intentions; to dispel all spells; to chase away fierce beasts and cause snakes to lose their poison. Everyone benefits from her benevolence.

I am convinced, at a deep subconscious level, that it was Kuan Yin who brought Lama Kyabje Zopa Rinpoche into my life, for the moment when we connected corresponded to a period when I was making heartfelt prayers to her for help. For some time I had been feeling that my life was rather meaningless, that all the success I was attaining was transient. I suspected there was more I could do to make my life worthwhile, if only I knew what to do and how to go about it. It was at around that time, when I turned inward, that I began my writing career. Then, a few months later, a fax came from a stranger – a lama I did not know and had never heard of. And so Rinpoche came into my life …

Chinese theologians who have undertaken research into the origins of this popular deity explain Kuan Yin as the female manifestation of the Compassion Buddha, Avalokiteshvara. Legends abound on her many manifestations in forms to which we can relate. Some date the transformation of Kuan Yin from male to female to the fifth century, during the time of the North–South dynasties of China.

The most popular tale concerning Kuan Yin's origin describes her as the beloved princess Miao Shan, whose virtuous purity at first angered her father, the king. But despite many obstacles and the fierce opposition placed in her path by him, in the end she succeeded in convincing her father to take the virtuous path toward enlightenment. She did this by cutting off her own arms and sacrificing her eyes to cure him of his illness.

The legend of Princess Miao Shan presents Kuan Yin as the beautiful, all-forgiving, all-compassionate princess and this is her most widespread manifestation. Dressed in white robes, and with a serene expression, she carries a small bottle of nectar in one hand and a fly whisk in the other, and is depicted sitting on a lotus, standing on a dragon, or on a tortoise crossing turbulent waters.

I love Kuan Yin in all her "thirty-three manifestations and fourteen bestowals of fearlessness," and these different images provide a wealth of inspiration for those who wish to practice her meditations. She is also depicted as a four-armed goddess, and this is the form to visualize when praying for courage. Finally, there is the image of the 1,000-armed Kuan Yin with sixteen heads. Each arm ends in a hand with an all-seeing eye, so that in this form Kuan Yin sees all, illuminates all, and helps all. This aspect embodies the union of compassion and wisdom that leads to enlightenment.

For as long as I can remember, I have viewed Kuan Yin as the embodiment of the Bodhisattva in all of us. The nearest equivalent in the Western tradition would be an angel – a good angel, someone who watches over you, invisible, powerful, and benevolent.

The root of your life problems becomes non-existent when you start to cherish others.

LAMA KYABJE ZOPA RINPOCHE

Prayer to Kuan Yin

The divine form of Kuan Yin is visualized, who is the embodiment of all the infinite buddhas' compassionate wisdom. She sits serenely on a beautiful lotus and white moon seat. From her body shines a halo of white light. She is youthful, and her head is covered with a lovely white robe that drapes her body. Kuan Yin is magnificently beautiful. One thinks:

I go for refuge until I am enlightened in the Buddha, Dharma, and Sangha. With the merit I create by practicing compassion and other perfections, may I attain buddhahood. In all my lives please be my virtuous friend. Show me the pure path that leads to enlightenment, and quickly place me in Buddha's state.

The famous six-syllable mantra of the Compassion Buddha, Om Mani Padme Hum is recited, while doing the meditation and visualization.

After every 108 recitations, white light is visualized coming from Kuan Yin, flowing into and completely filling the whole body. It purifies selfishness, the self-cherishing mind, ignorance, attachment, and anger – obstacles to a person's practice of compassion. The white light blesses the person practicing the visualization, and gives them the ability to understand and integrate kindness in their daily lives. They dedicate their prayers to attaining the bodhichitta heart – the intense wish to attain enlightenment for the sake of all sentient beings.

Compassion is the best healer. The most powerful healing comes from developing compassion for all living beings.

LAMA KYABJE ZOPA RINPOCHE

Prayer wheels are inscribed with the mantra Om Mani Padme Hum, the mantra of Kuan Yin, Chenrezig, and Avalokiteshvara, all forms of the Compassion Buddha.

Meditation on 1,000-armed Chenrezig

The heart and mind are focussed on the thought of taking refuge in the Triple Gem: the Buddha, Dharma (Buddha's teachings), and Sangha (the ordained community of monks and nuns). If the person practicing the meditation has a guru, he or she takes refuge first in him and then in the Triple Gem. The following verse is recited three times:

I go for refuge until I am enlightened, to the Buddha, Dharma, and Sangha. By the positive potential I create by practicing bodhichitta and the other perfections, may I attain buddhahood, for the sake of all sentient beings.

The divine form of 1,000-armed Chenrezig is visualized, the embodiment of all the infinite buddhas' compassionate wisdom.

The Four Immeasurable Thoughts are generated three times (see page 22), then motivation is generated by reciting the following:

The purpose of my life is to free all sentient beings from suffering, to bring them happiness, especially full enlightenment. Therefore I must become a Buddha, I must gain full enlightenment and possess perfect qualities, the omniscient mind, the power to reveal various methods, and the perfect compassion embracing the numberless living beings.

Therefore I must actualize the stages of the path to enlightenment.

Especially for the sake of all mother sentient beings, I must quickly and more quickly – in this very life – attain the precious state of complete and perfect buddhahood.

Therefore I shall practice the graduated path of Buddha Chenrezig yoga.

The seven-limbed prayer is recited (see page 116), the mandala offering is made (see page 252), the request prayer is recited, then the meditation on the Eight Verses of Thought Transformation.

Standing on a lotus and moon seat, Chenrezig's body is in the form of white light, youthful and decorated with magnificent jewel ornaments.

REQUEST PRAYER

O Arya, compassionate-eyed One, who is the treasure of compassion,
I request you, please listen to me. Please guide myself, and all my mothers
    and fathers,
In all six realms to be freed quickly from the great ocean of samsara.
I request that the vast and profound peerless awakening mind may grow.
With the tear of your great compassion, please cleanse all karmas
    and delusion.
Please with your hand of compassion lead me and all pitiful migrators to
    fields of bliss.
Please, Amitabha and Chenrezig, in all my lives be virtuous friends.
Show well the undeceptive pure path and quickly place us in Buddha's
    enlightened state.

THE EIGHT VERSES OF THOUGHT TRANSFORMATION

These verses are excellent for mind-training, and it is important to meditate on each verse with the sincere motivation of generating compassion. I have heard Lama Kyabje Zopa Rinpoche urge this many times. I have also attended teachings from His Holiness the Dalai Lama when he has said that these verses are most helpful in generating bodhichitta. After each verse, one visualizes light coming from Chenrezig, flowing into them, and filling their whole body. It purifies the selfishness and ignorance that prevent an understanding of the meaning of the verse, and gives the ability to integrate each verse into daily life. After reading each verse out loud, one mala (108 repeats) of the OM MANI PADME HUM mantra can be recited, while simultaneously visualizing Chenrezig. This helps gain the blessings of Avalokiteshvara that lead to realizations and understanding.

1. Determined to obtain the greatest possible benefit from all sentient beings, who are more precious than a wish-fulfilling jewel, I shall hold them most dear at all times.
   OM MANI PADME HUM

2. When in the company of others, I shall always consider myself as the lowest of all, and from the depths of my heart hold others dear and supreme.
   OM MANI PADME HUM

3. Vigilant, the moment a delusion appears in my mind, endangering myself and others, I shall confront and avert it without delay.
   OM MANI PADME HUM

4. Whenever I see beings who are wicked in nature and who are overwhelmed by violent negative actions and suffering, I shall hold such rare ones dear, as if I had found a precious treasure.
   OM MANI PADME HUM

5. When out of envy others mistreat me with abuse, insults or the like, I shall accept defeat and offer the victory to others.
   OM MANI PADME HUM

6. When someone whom I have benefited and in whom I have placed great hope gives me terrible harm I shall regard that person as my holy guru.
   OM MANI PADME HUM

7. In short, both directly and indirectly, do I offer every happiness and benefit to all my mothers. I shall secretly take upon myself all their harmful actions and sufferings.
   OM MANI PADME HUM

8. Undefiled by the stains of the superstitions of the Eight World concerns [explain] may I, by perceiving all phenomena as illusory, be released from the bondage of attachment.
   OM MANI PADME HUM

CHENREZIG'S PURIFICATION MEDITATION AND LONG MANTRA RECITATION

Chenrezig is visualized as coming to the top of one's head, facing the same direction. He is then seen on the heads of all the sentient beings who are seated around. At each of Chenrezig's hearts, a lotus and flat moon disk are visualized. At the center of the moon is the seed-syllable HRIH, the essence of Chenrezig's wisdom and compassion, surrounded by mantras. From the mantras, white light, and HRIH, nectar – the nature of Chenrezig's sentient mind – flows into the body, blissfully purifying all delusions, negative karmic imprints, diseases, and obscurations. Similarly, light and nectar purify the negativities and obscurations of all sentient beings. The visualization is performed while this long mantra is recited twenty-eight times:

NAMO RATNA TRA YA YA
NAMA ARYA JNANA SAGARA
VAIROCHANA BVYUHA RAJAYA
TATHAGATAYA, ARHATE SAMYAKSAM BUDDHAYA

NAMA SARVA TATHAGATE BHYA
ARHATE BHYAH SAMYAKSAM BUDDHE BHYAH

NAMA ARYA AVALOKITESH VARAYA
BODHISATVAYA
MAHA SATTVAYA
MAHA KARUNIKAYA

TADYATHA
OM DHARA DHARA
DHIRI DHIRI DHURU DHURU
ITTE VATTE CHALE CHALE
PRACHALE PRACHALE KUSUME KUSUME VARE
ILI MILI CITI JVALAM APANAYE SVAHA

One thinks the following:

From now on, I will live my life in a meaningful way and do all actions with the motivation to attain enlightenment for the benefit of all sentient beings.

Because I have a noble intention, Chenrezig is extremely pleased. He melts into white light and absorbs into my heart. Through Chenrezig absorbing into me, my mind becomes the nature of great compassion, loving-kindness, and bodhichitta. My body is filled with light and becomes very pure and clear, like crystal.

Chenrezig is then visualized on the heads of all sentient beings, melting into light and being absorbed into them. Chenrezig blesses them so that they may progress along the gradual path to enlightenment. Next, the prayers below are recited in order to dedicate the positive potential of the meditation:

Due to this merit, may I soon attain the enlightened state of Chenrezig, that I may be able to liberate all sentient beings from their suffering. May the precious bodhi mind not yet born arise and grow. May that mind that is born have no decline, but increase for evermore.

Due to the positive potential accumulated by myself and others in the past, present, and future, may anyone who merely sees, hears, remembers, touches, or talks to me be freed in that very instant from all sufferings and abide in happiness for ever.

In all my rebirths, may I and all sentient beings be born into a good family, have clear wisdom, have great compassion, be free of pride and devoted to our Spiritual Masters, and abide within our vows and commitments.

In whatever guise you appear, O Chenrezig, whatever your retinue, your lifespan, and Pure Land, whatever your name, most noble and holy, may I and all others attain only these.

By the force of these praises and requests made to you, may all disease, poverty, fighting, and quarrels be calmed. May all wars cease. May harmony prevail throughout the world. May the Dharma and all auspiciousness increase throughout the world and in all the directions where I and all others dwell.

DAILY ACTIVITIES

When a person is going about their daily activities, they can visualize a small radiant Chenrezig, at their heart. This hels them to be mindful of their actions, for Chenrezig is a witness to all that is said and done during the day. Whenever one eats or enjoys other pleasures, it is imagined that these are offered to Chenrezig; if a person is praised, rather than becoming proud, he or she thinks that others are, praising Chenrezig.

Generating bodhichitta is a special attitude, embodying the fervent wish to attain enlightenment for the purpose of benefiting others. Without this wish, it is impossible to attain enlightenment. In fact, as long as someone thinks habitually in a selfish way, there is no opportunity even for temporal happiness. The Eight Verses on Thought Transformation (see page 150) are easy to memorize. They have immense power to turn all the difficult people in our lives into precious teachers. This change in attitude is a skilful and effective way to deal with people who annoy us or make us unhappy. It is essential in attaining both temporal happiness and ultimate enlightenment. It is a stunning method for transforming problems into happiness, and a powerful tool for healing.

A VISUALIZATION FOR PROSTRATIONS

Lama Zopa says making procrastinations to Chenrezig is equivalent to making prostrations to all the Buddhas. When a person makes prostrations to Avalokiteshvara, white nectar is visualized flowing from this buddha's heart, and he or she imagines that that all the obscurations of their body, speech, and mind are completely purified. It is like turning on a flashlight in a dark room: the darkness disappears instantly. One technique to help with this practice is to imagine that total darkness represents all the obstacles that prevent the attainment of realization; then Chenrezig sends blessings and realizations in the form of white light. In this way all the three doors of the body, speech, and mind are purified and become one with Avalokiteshvara. If this visualization can be achieved, it purifies a great many negative karmas.

As a person stretches out on the floor to make a prostration, they visualize a replica of Avalokiteshvara being absorbed into them. It is like lighting a candle from another candle: the original flame is still there, but when a second candle is lit, another flame emerges from it.

The lighting of candles at pujas represents the attainment of blessings and realizations that shine through the darkness of the obscured mind.

6

All the faults of our mind are temporary, not permanent and everlasting; and so our suffering is also temporary.

LAMA KYABJE ZOPA RINPOCHE

The Trinity of Longevity Buddhas: White Tara, Amitayus, and Namgyalma

The gift of longevity

There is a beautiful trinity of buddhas who, individually and collectively, bestow the precious gift of longevity. The trinity comprises the serenely matriarchal White Tara, the powerfully compassionate Buddha Amitayus, and the mysterious Namgyalma – an emanation of the Buddha Vairochana. These are the buddhas who help us overcome karmic obstacles, serious danger, and unexpected threats to our life. In order to cheat the Lord of Death and be rescued from succumbing to fatal illnesses and accidents that might cause premature death, it is beneficial to become acquainted with at least one of these Longevity buddhas.

When you look at life from a spiritual perspective, you will understand that there is only one reason for wanting to have a long life: to prolong your precious human existence, so that you have more time to create the cause for positive advancement along the spiritual path to enlightenment. This means living a life that is as beneficial to as many beings as possible. This is especially true for high lamas: the longer they live, the more thousands of people they can benefit. It is for this reason that Buddhists are so fond of organizing long-life pujas (religious offering ceremonies) dedicated to their high lamas, and especially to His Holiness the Dalai Lama.

White Tara with Buddha Amitayus (bottom left) and Buddha Namglyalma (bottom right). Shakyamuni Buddha can be seen top center.

Long-life pujas

I have attended several long-life pujas and they are incredibly moving occasions. The air is filled with a special energy, created by the heartfelt praises and specially composed prayers that are addressed to the lama, who sits on a throne dressed in his ritual robes and hat in all their splendor. At my first such puja, held in Kopan monastery for my precious guru, Lama Kyabje Zopa Rinpoche (who is also the high lama of Kopan), I was amazed at the spectacle laid out in the big gompa or prayer hall. There must have been at least 2,000 monks, nuns, and lay people wanting to bring offerings to their dearly beloved lama. Rinpoche really looked like a king – a Dharma king – and I felt as if I had gone back in time to another century and another place. The sense of déjà vu was compelling.

The long-life puja is not unlike a mass, and I was lucky in that I had a monk seated next to me explaining and translating. First there are ritual prayers, chanted by the monks accompanied by ancient drums and other instruments. And while the prayers are going on, tsog offerings of butter tea, rice, biscuits, and fruit are distributed to celebrate the occasion. About halfway through the ritual occurs the dramatic entrance of six dakinis – supposedly, fairy maidens from the Pure Land who have come down to the human realm to entice the lama back with them. They are dressed in elaborate embroidered robes and headdresses.

The dance of the dakinis is highly ritualistic. The beat of the sacred instruments is hypnotic, and is interspersed with occasional bursts of sound from the conch shell, as it gets blown by the young monks. The dance is meaningful when you understand the gestures and the way in which the robes swish extravagantly as the dakinis dance in front of the lama. All the while, the monks are chanting prayers; it is an amazing dramatic spectacle.

Many offerings and praises are heaped on the dakinis to encourage them to return to their land, accepting that they have failed to persuade the lama to go with them. As the dakinis leave, you can sense a lightness in the air, for their flight from the gompa signals their lack of success in enticing the lama back to the Pure Land.

As the puja draws to an end, devotees form a long line to make offerings to the lama. This part of the ceremony is truly something to watch and can take at least as long as the first part. The offerings comprise every variety of auspicious and holy objects, paintings, buddha statues decorated with precious stones, brocades, Longevity buddhas, and so forth. Everyone lines up with an offering, for it is believed to be auspicious to give such a gift to the guru.

When I was in the queue making my offering to Rinpoche that first time, a sense of gratitude took hold of me as I bowed low and handed over my offering tray, on which lay a golden Dharmachakra – the Dharma wheel symbolizing Rinpoche giving us teachings. I felt suddenly close to tears as I realized in that instant how truly precious Rinpoche's life had become for me.

Since then I have attended various long-life pujas for Lama Kyabje Zopa Rinpoche and other lamas, and each time the same feeling takes hold of me. No matter how elaborate or how simple the puja is, the experience is the same: a realization of just how precious life is. It is vital to appreciate this, so that we do not take our lives for granted, or waste them by making the pursuit of meaningless pleasures (which benefit neither ourselves nor others) the central pillar of our existence.

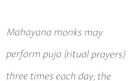

Mahayana monks may perform puja (ritual prayers) three times each day; the precious intent of each ritual is never taken for granted.

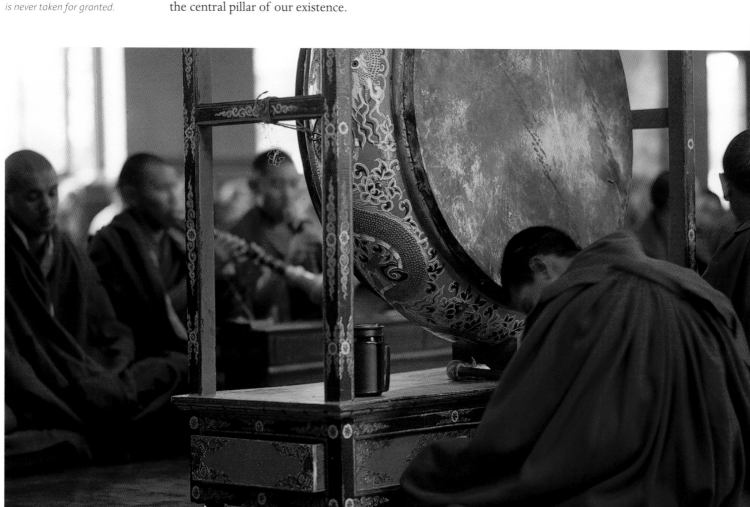

THE PRECIOUSNESS OF HUMAN REBIRTH

With the realization of the preciousness of human rebirth comes the conviction that it is vital to prolong our lives as much as possible. In fact, for Tibetan Buddhists who follow the tradition of His Holiness the Dalai Lama – the Gelug tradition – the Lam-Rim, or graduated path to enlightenment, is like a Bible. Meditations on the Lam-Rim offer a step-by-step approach in the quest for enlightenment. Moving along this path may take many lifetimes, and we each have our own personal flow and rhythm when it comes to progressing along it. However, it is important to make a start …

The Lam-Rim has been described as "liberation in the palm of your hand." Probably the greatest translated text on this subject is the treatise based on the retreat teachings of one of the most eminent high lamas of Tibet, His Holiness Pabongka Rinpoche. The title of this extensive work is also Liberation in the Palm of Your Hand. I have to say that it is not a book for cursory reading: it is a difficult work and needs to be read, meditated upon, and read again and again. I have been reading it for the past five years, and I am still at the beginning. For those of you interested in knowing exactly what the path to liberation is, the Lam-Rim meditation prayer is included overleaf. You will find that the root of the path is the guru, for without a guru it is impossible to make progress. The first realization is thus to find and recognize your guru, and then to practice guru devotion.

The Lam-Rim opens the door to Tantric Buddhism, which is the quick path to enlighten-ment. What would normally take a billion years may now take a single lifetime. Thus libera-tion from the karmic cycle of birth, death, and rebirth is placed in your own hands.

Next comes the meditation on the preciousness of human rebirth – of human life itself. For taking birth as a human being is so rare that it is said in the sutras that the probability of human rebirth is even less than finding a tortoise in the middle of the ocean with a golden ring around its neck! The second realization is thus to know how very precious your life is.

Making offerings to buddhas reaffirms the precious nature of the lives of all beings, and celebrates the gifts that buddhas bestow, including long life.

LAM-RIM MEDITATION AND PRAYER

The following Lam-Rim meditation and prayer is by Lama Tsongkhapa, entitled "The Foundation of All Good Qualities". It asks for blessings to gain the realizations that lead to enlightenment.

The foundation of all good qualities is the kind and venerable guru;
Correct devotion to him is the root of the path.
By clearly seeing this and applying great effort,
Please bless me to rely upon him with great respect.

Understanding that the precious freedom of this rebirth is found only once,
Is greatly meaningful, and is difficult to find again,
Please bless me to generate the mind that unceasingly,
Day and night, takes its essence.

This life is as impermanent as a water bubble;
Remember how quickly it decays and death comes.
After death, just like a shadow follows the body,
The results of black and white karma follow.

Finding firm and definite conviction in this,
Please bless me always to be careful
To abandon even the slightest negativities
And accomplish all virtuous deeds.

Seeking samsaric pleasures is the door to all suffering:
They are uncertain and cannot be relied upon.
Recognizing these shortcomings,
Please bless me to generate the strong wish for the bliss of liberation.

Led by this pure thought,
Mindfulness, alertness, and great caution arise.
The root of the teachings is keeping the pratimoksha vows:
Please bless me to accomplish this essential practice.

Just as I have fallen into the sea of samsara,
So have all mother migratory beings.
Please bless me to see this, train in supreme bodhichitta,
And bear the responsibility of freeing migratory beings.

Even if I develop only bodhichitta, but I don't practice the three types of morality,
I will not achieve enlightenment.
With my clear recognition of this,
Please bless me to practice the bodhisattva vows with great energy.

Once I have pacified distractions to wrong objects
And correctly analyzed the meaning of reality,
Please bless me to generate quickly within my mindstream
The unified path of calm abiding and special insight.

Having become a pure vessel by training in the general path,
Please bless me to enter
The holy gateway of the fortunate ones:
The supreme vajra vehicle.

At that time, the basis of accomplishing the two attainments
Is keeping pure vows and samaya.
As I have become firmly convinced of this,
Please bless me to protect these vows and pledges like my life.

Then, having realized the importance of the two stages,
The essence of the Vajrayana,
By practicing with great energy, never giving up the four sessions,
Please bless me to realize the teachings of the holy guru.

Like that, may the gurus who show the noble path
And the spiritual friends who practice it have long lives.
Please bless me to pacify completely
All outer and inner hindrances.

In all my lives, never separated from perfect gurus,
May I enjoy the magnificent Dharma.
By completing the qualities of the stages and paths,
May I quickly attain the state of Vajradhara.

If you are reading about the Lam-Rim for the first time, many of the references to the gradu-ated path to enlightenment may seem strange to you. They did to me, too, when I started … But what I did was simply remain at the early stages of the Lam-Rim. I am doing this at my own pace and according to my own flow, so I do not allow myself to rush. You can do the same. The most important thing is to open your heart to finding a guru, if you do not already have one. If you do have a guru, let this book merely serve as a catalyst for you to gain the first realization. All other things will follow from there! Including the practices of the Longevity buddhas.

Lama Tsongkhapa in the
main gompa (prayer hall) at
Kopan monastery, Nepal.

Meeting White Tara

White Tara is a female buddha of long life, and she is incredibly beautiful. Every painting I have ever seen of her has taken my breath away. There is something stunningly peaceful and reassuring about her expression. She is a mother figure, with one face and two hands, seated in the posture of the vajra (thunderbolt) above a white moon disk and an open lotus.

White Tara's aura glows, as various colored rings framed with pink lotus blossoms surround her. Her garments are elaborately decorated with ornaments; on her head she wears a sparkling tiara; and she is adorned with beautiful jewelry – a long and short necklace, as well as various gold and jewel ornaments. Her right hand rests across her knee in the mudra of supreme generosity, while her left hand holds near her heart the stem of a uptala flower, which is blossoming near her left ear. White Tara is always depicted as a peaceful deity.

The easiest way to recognize her is to look for her distinguishing marks: her seven eyes and, of course, her great beauty. There are three eyes on her face (including one on her forehead) and one eye on each palm of her hands and feet. It is said that White Tara's seven eyes enable her to clearly "see" all beings in all the realms of existence. Her expression is one of the utmost compassion. Her hand mudras are similar to those of Green Tara (see page 174), but she is seated cross-legged rather than in the ready-to-rise pose of Green Tara.

Her sadhana helps practitioners to overcome life-threatening obstacles. To overcome the power of the Lord of Death, you can do her spiritual practice, recite her mantras, and focus on a successful visualization of her wish-fulfilling wheel. White Tara practice can also be done on someone else's behalf. For instance, if you have a loved one fighting for his or her life in hospital, you can recite the White Tara mantra and perform the practice and visualizations. It is an excellent idea to hang a picture of White Tara in your home, as this is believed to automatically invoke her blessings.

Many practitioners regard White Tara as the longevity-bestowing aspect of Green Tara. She belongs to the Kriya class of Tantra , but all schools of Tibetan Buddhism, whether old or new, practice White Tara.

Once, Lama Kyabje Zopa Rinpoche wanted to thank a friend of mine who had done us a favor by helping some monks from India get their visas approved urgently. Rinpoche carefully selected a stunning White Tara thangka for him, and my friend hung it in his study at home. Several months later I heard that he had had a mild heart attack and that his wife and family were extremely worried. I advised him to make daily water-bowl offerings to the thangka of White Tara, as I was convinced that his timely favor concerning the visas was a karmic occurrence, which created the cause for the entrée of White Tara into his consciousness. Thankfully, he recovered and today enjoys a measure of good health. It is hard to believe that a mere image can cause remarkable cures to take place, but I am told there are many stories and legends that attest to the power of holy images.

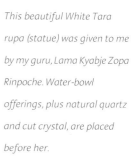

This beautiful White Tara rupa (statue) was given to me by my guru, Lama Kyabje Zopa Rinpoche. Water-bowl offerings, plus natural quartz and cut crystal, are placed before her.

LONG-LIFE WHITE TARA PRACTICE

This very short practice was given to me by Rinpoche. It is easy to perform, and takes only a few minutes. First, motivation is generated: that practicing White Tara's longevity meditation is not just for oneself, but especially for the benefit of all sentient beings. Prior to any special meditation and visualization, it is always a good idea to spend a few moments generating a compassionate motivation and calming the mind. Then, from the heart, refuge is taken in the Buddha, Dharma, and Sangha, and prostrations are made to White Tara.

The person doing the White Tara practice visualizes the seed-syllable "Tam" above their head or in front of them, at the height of their forehead. From the Tam, White Tara emerges: beautiful and smiling, surrounded by many buddhas and by the other two Longevity buddhas, Amitayus and Namgyalma.

Long-life nectar is imagined coming from Tara's heart. This blissful white-light energy enters the crown of the person's head, and fills their body. They feel strongly that all negative karma, obscurations, spirit harm, and sicknesses are being completely purified. This meditative visualization is best done while chanting White Tara's mantra.

WHITE TARA'S MANTRA

OM TARE TUTTARE TURE MAMA AYUR PUNYE
JNYANA PUSHTIM KURU YE SVAHA.

While reciting one mala (108 repeats), one concentrates on the nectar entering and filling their body. This is White Tara passing the nectar of longevity. When one mala has been completed, the practitioner senses keenly that their lifespan has been increased, their merit has developed, scriptural understanding and wisdom have been enhanced, and life is becoming ever more meaningful for all sentient beings. Above all, they focus on feeling that they are attaining many precious realizations. Before getting up, the merit obtained from making the White Tara sadhana is dedicated to the attainment of enlightenment for the sake of all sentient beings.

Meeting Buddha Amitayus

The Buddha Amitayus is regarded as the longevity-granting aspect of Buddha Amitabha. Both of these buddhas have a red body, but their mudras and symbols are different. Amitayus is recognized by the vase that he holds in his two hands, which are in the mudra of meditation. The vase contains the precious nectar of longevity, which fills up and overflows each time you do the Amitayus practice and sadhana. While Amitabha is the Buddha of Infinite Light, Amitayus is the Buddha of Infinite Life. His practice is said to be extremely powerful, not merely in dissolving life obstacles (which may cause death), but in overcoming the obscurations that lead to suffering and to a lack of progress along the spiritual path.

Once, out of the blue, Lama Kyabje Zopa Rinpoche sent me the precious mantras of Amitayus, together with advice on how to do his practice. Three times – in Kopan, in Taiwan, and in Singapore – he had presented me with statues of Amitayus and I had been so blind that I had not realized their significance and had not asked for Amitayus' practice. But Rinpoche is amazingly kind and very clairvoyant. Tibetan Buddhists believe that when you come under the care of a lama, it represents great good fortune, for he will always be looking after you, even though you may be unaware of it. I can attest to this, because Rinpoche must have seen some pretty big life obstacles in that period of my life, so he sent me the powerful mantras of Amitayus, and I now share this practice here.

Amitayus exists to grant long life to all sentient beings.

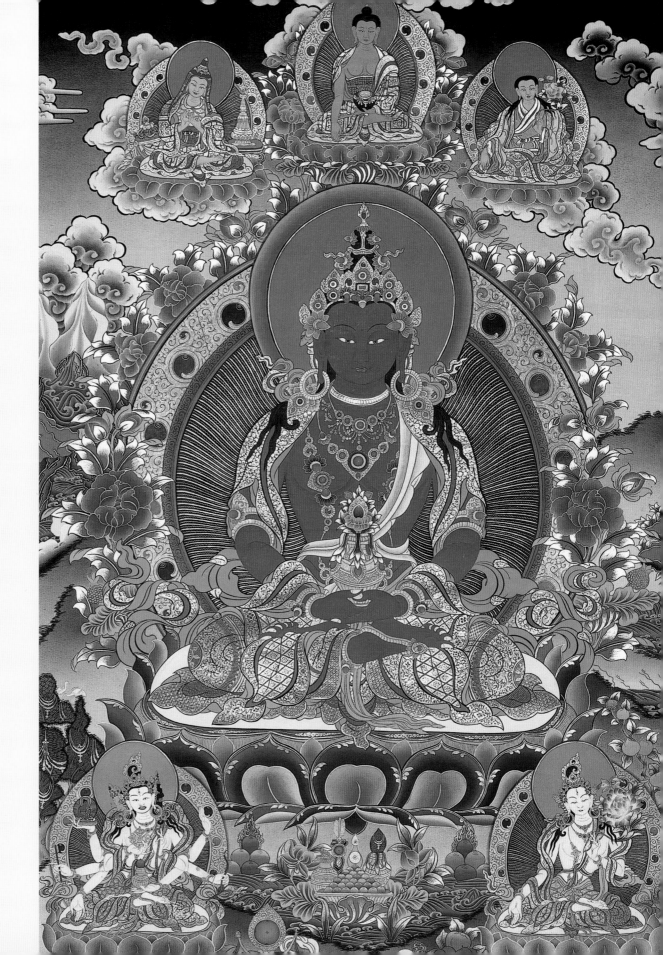

LONG-LIFE MEDITATION OF BUDDHA AMITAYUS

Three prostrations are made to Buddha Amitayus, and refuge is taken in the Buddha, Dharma, and Sangha. Just above the crown a lotus, and on that a moon disk, are visualized. Above this appears Amitayus, who embodies all the transcendental wisdom that sees all past, present, and future existences, and all the perfect power of the buddhas.

Red Amitayus is visualized, with one face and two hands. He is holding a long-life vase, and his legs are crossed in the vajra position. Amitayus is in the sambhogakaya aspect, having the thirty-two major and 108 minor signs of a Buddha. At his heart are a lotus and moon disk, and the seed-syllable HRIH stands in the center of the moon disk, symbolizing the holy mind of the Infinite Life Buddha.

Beams of red light emit from the HRIH in all directions. They draw forth the essence of the earth, water, fire, and air elements, which is then absorbed into and fills up the vase held in Amitayus' hands. They also draw forth all the long life of the great yogis and holy beings, including the buddhas – those who have achieved undying life, such as arhats and bodhisattvas – and this enters the vase in the form of white light and nectar. Then all of a person's life that has been stolen away by spirits or harmed by black magic (all the essence of life in samsara) is drawn forth, and fills the vase in the form of nectar.

This long-life nectar overflows from the vase and enters the crown chakra of a person's head, then flows into all the body's psychic channels, blessing the whole mind and body. Amitayus' powerful nectar purifies all disease, spirit harms, negative karmas, and obscurations that have plagued us all this time.

All mental obscurations and negative karma pour out of every pore of the body in the form of dirty black liquid. All diseases and allergies are released in the form of blood and pus; and all spirit harms leave the body as black scorpions, frogs, and snakes.

While visualizing this, the mantra of Amitayus (overleaf) is recited at least three times, and ideally seven times.

An array of prayer hangings depicting Tara buddhas.

THE MANTRA OF AMITAYUS

NAMO RATNA TRA YAYA / OM NAMO BHAGAVATE
APARIMITA AYUR JNYANA
SUPINISH CHITATAYE
JORA JAYA/TATHAGATAYA
ARHATE SAMYAKSAM BUDDHAYA/TA YA THA
OM PUNYE PUNYE / MAHA PUNYE
APARIMITA PUNYE
AYU PUNYE / MAHA PUNYE / AYUR JNYANA
SARVA RUPA SIDDHI
AYUR JNYANA KAY CHE BHRUM
OM BHRUM / AH BHRUM
SVA BHRUM / HA BHRUM / CHE BHRUM
OM SARVA SAMSKARA
PARI SHUDDHA DHARMATAY
GAGANA SAMUDGATE
SVABHAVA VISHUDDHE
MAHA NAYA PARIVARA YE SVAHA

THE SHORT MANTRA OF AMITAYUS

If desired, the mantra above can be followed with one mala (108 repeats) of the short mantra of Amitayus.

OM AMARANI JIVAN TIYE SVAHA

This is the essence of all the Transcendental Inconceivable Life

There are immeasurable benefits to be gained from reciting this mantra, even once. The merit is described as being more supreme than that obtained from making images of the holy buddhas in gold, silver, or copper, and with the precious jewels of the three galaxies. Reciting it results in the yogi not experiencing any of the eight aspects of death. All inauspicious signs and bad omens are stopped, and one is able to eliminate hundreds of obstacles. Due to the blessings gained from reciting this mantra, all obstacles and sicknesses are removed and all auspiciousness is received. However, even the buddhas and their princes, the bodhisattvas, are unable to express fully all the benefits of this mantra. The ultimate reality of it is the sound of itself.

Lama Kyabje Zopa Rinpoche in Bodhgaya, India, 2001.

Meeting Namgyalma

The third of the longevity trinity is the cosmic Buddha Namgyalma, who is sometimes referred to as Ushnisha Vijaya. She belongs to the family of Buddha Vairochana – one of the five Dhyani buddhas (see Chapter 2). Her practice is reputed to be extremely powerful, not only in eliminating the obstacles to long life but in purifying all negative actions of body, speech, and mind.

Namgyalma has a white body, three faces, and eight arms. The face in the center is white and has a gentle, compassionate expression. The right face is yellow, with a peaceful-wrathful expression, and the left face is blue, with a wrathful expression. Each face has three eyes.

Namgyalma's eight arms hold several meaningful symbols. The first right arm clutches a crossed vajra (thunderbolt); the second right arm holds a lotus, on which Amitabha is seated; the third holds an arrow; and the fourth is in the mudra of bestowing blessings. The four left hands seem to signify the wrathful face of Namgyalma: the first hand is in the mudra of fearlessness; the second is in the mudra of giving refuge; the third holds a noose; and the fourth holds in her lap a vase filled with nectar.

The choice of which Longevity buddhas to worship is a personal matter between a practitioner and his or her spiritual guru. It is essential to note that all three Longevity buddhas are extremely powerful cosmic buddhas, and it is always wise to get advice from a qualified guru and to ask them for oral transmissions of the mantras, or even request an initiation. This is like being given permission to do the practices and recite the mantras, and it enhances their effectiveness and power.

A Dharma connection is established the moment you make the decision that someone is your own guru ... and on the basis of this determination, receive even one verse of teaching or the oral transmission of a few syllables of mantra ...

LAMA KYABJE ZOPA RINPOCHE

THE MANTRA OF NAMGYALMA

Recite one mala (108 repeats) of the short mantra of Namgyalma:

OM BHRUM SVAHA
OM AMRITA AYUR DA DAY SVAH

This representation of Namgyalma has three gold faces, with three visible hands holding the bow, the arrow, and Buddha Amitayus, on a lotus. The the fourth visible hand is in the mudra of fearlessness.

7

You can have whatever happiness of this life

you wish for ... simply by doing the twenty-one

Tara praises and reciting Tara mantras.

LAMA KYABJE ZOPA RINPOCHE

Meeting Green Tara, Mother Goddess

GREEN TARA'S HOLY MANTRA

OM TARE TUTTARE TURE SVAHA

There are many beautiful and inspiring recordings of Green Tara's mantra. If you come upon any of these musical mantras, sung by voices that seem to come from heaven, then playing them continuously in your home generates fantastic benefits. Everyone listening to the mantra – whether consciously or subconsciously – will receive the imprint of this wonderful goddess. And then at some stage in this life, or in a future life, this seed will ripen magnificently and you will actively invite Tara into your life. Rinpoche has explained the meaning of the Tara mantra as follows.

"Tare" means liberation from samsara. This samsara refers to the five impure aggregates of the body and mind. These five aggregates are form (the physical body); feeling; recognition; consciousness; and mental thoughts – and collectively they give rise to the conviction of existence, and of life itself. The Four Noble Truths tell us that life is in the nature of suffering, and because of delusions and negative karma created and accumulated through thousands of lifetimes, we are "stuck in a cycle of continuous birth and rebirth" – and this is samsara. Tare indicates that Mother Tara liberates us from this cycle of samsara and in so doing, liberates us instantaneously from the sufferings of birth, old age, sickness, and death; meeting undesirable objects and experiencing fear; not finding desirable objects; and not getting lasting satisfaction, even when we obtain desired objects. Tare liberates us from this cycle of dissatisfaction and suffering.

"Tuttare" liberates us from the eight fears. These refer to eight external dangers: lions, elephants, fire, serpents, thieves, prison chains, floods, and demons. They correspond to eight dangerous thoughts: pride, anger, envy, avarice, wrong views, attachments, doubt, and delusion. Taking refuge in Tara liberates us from them.

The left hand mudra of Green Tara is the three jewels giving refuge.

"Ture" liberates us from disease, which means not just physical disease but also mental disease, the afflictions of the subdued, disturbed mind; and the negative actions this creates. Thus she leads us to cessation of suffering (one of the Four Noble Truths, see page 23). This cessation is the ultimate. Our chief mental sickness is ignorance.

"Svaha" means establishing the root of the path in the heart. So by taking refuge in Tara, saying her mantras and chanting her praises, we receive her blessings, which purify all that is impure in us. Body, speech, and mind are transformed into Tara's holy body, speech, and mind. This is signified by the initial syllable, Om.

It seems then that the whole path to enlightenment is contained in the mantra Om Tare Tuttare Ture. This mantra also removes all obstacles toward understanding Dharma. Simultaneously, the mantra reflects the Lam-Rim meditation (see page 156–158) which differentiates between the lower, middle, and higher capability being. Thus Tare is the graduated path of the lower capable being; Tuttare is that of the middle capable being; and Ture that of the higher capable being.

Red Tara buddha at Bhaktapur, Nepal. This buddha transmits the power of persuasion. By chanting her mantra daily – Om Ah Tare Tuttare Ture Washen Kuru So Ha – you can request blessings that will enhance your persuasive skills.

Tara, mother of all the buddhas

In the entire Universe, there is none like mother Tara. She is the emanation of all the buddhas' miraculous enlightened activities, transcending times past, present, and future. Tara is the wisdom-mother of all the buddhas. She manifests both peaceful and wrathful aspects and appears in different colors – red, black, white, golden, yellow, orange, and green. It is as the Green Tara that she is most widely known, and from her emanate the twenty-one Taras in different aspects, each with a special mantra and a specific miraculous energy. You can pray to mother Tara for almost anything, for she is the ultimate solace for all who seek help, comfort, and solutions to their problems. She is the one we can turn to when there is no one else. And the path to enlightenment becomes that much smoother when we call on her for blessings to guide us along the way …

Much has been written about this wonderful goddess who holds such a special place in the hearts of Buddhists. They know that taking refuge in Tara – simply entering beneath her right-hand mudra, which grants refuge – anyone in need of her protection is instantly safe-guarded from every fear. The mantra of Green Tara – Om Tare Tuttare Ture Svaha – is almost as popular as the six-syllable Om Mani Padme Hum mantra of Avalokiteshvara (see page 128). Indeed, Tara is said to have arisen from the lake of compassionate tears shed by Avalokiteshvara. Thus, from the very instant of her cosmic birth, Tara became the essence of compassion and vowed to remove the suffering of all sentient beings and to lead them to enlightenment. She is thus the manifestation of all the buddhas' liberating activity.

Tara belongs to two buddha families. She is the consort of Buddha Amoghasiddhi, the green-colored cosmic buddha of the North, but she was born of Avalokiteshvara, and so belongs to Amitabha's Lotus family. The meaning of the word Tara is "savioress", and in Tibetan her name is Drolma.

Tara's origin as the "mother of the Tathagatas," or mother of the buddhas, comes from India, and she was popularized in Tibet by the great Indian scholar Lama Atisha (982–1054). He was described as being so devoted to the goddess that his affection communicated itself to everyone with whom he came in contact. Much of Tara's appeal comes from the speed of results associated with her practice, for she is the swift heroine. So the praises to Tara begin, "Homage! Tara, swift, heroic …" Hers is the fast route to wisdom and enlightenment.

Those wanting children, by doing Tara prayers and mantras will have children. Those wanting a son will get a son; those wanting a daughter will get a daughter.

LAMA KYABJE ZOPA RINPOCHE

Answering every prayer

Of all the forms of Tara, the two most popular and well known are those of the Green Tara and the White Tara. Green Tara is the mother-liberator who answers every prayer, while White Tara is the goddess who grants extended life (see page 162). Tibetans believe that the Chinese and Nepalese wives of their Buddhist king Songtsen Gampo were emanations of two forms of Tara – the Chinese bride was said to be Green Tara, and the queen from Nepal, White Tara. They were instrumental in establishing Buddhism in the king's court.

The most popular prayer to Tara is the famous "Praises to the Twenty-One Taras" (see page 198). It is believed that those who recite these praises wisely and piously, and with the fullest faith in the goddess, are certain to have all their aspirations fulfilled. Those wanting wealth will find wealth; those wanting to conceive will do so; those wanting realizations will be showered with a rainfall of blessings; and so on.

In the five years since I first met Lama Kyabje Zopa Rinpoche, he has explained many aspects of Tara practices to me. Most importantly, he has kindly given me oral transmissions of several of her mantras. The most significant milestone in my personal practice to this wonderful goddess came when I was lucky enough to receive the Green Tara initiation from Rinpoche. It happened during one of my annual visits to Kopan monastery to participate in part of the month-long meditation retreat and attend teachings given by Rinpoche. On one such retreat I was filled with a great yearning to do serious Tara practice, so I humbly requested the Green Tara initiation from Rinpoche.

At workshops at Patan, Nepal,
Tara statues are cast by hand
and individually assembled.

Requesting initiation from a high lama who holds the lineage empowers your practice of the buddha-deity. But whether you succeed in getting the initiation depends as much on your karma as on the intensity of your desire. On that occasion Rinpoche nodded, and later when it was announced that there would be a Green Tara initiation we were all very excited. I am not alone in feeling drawn to this goddess. Many people who discover the Buddhist path feel the same kind of affinity.

On the evening of the appointed day, we all gathered in the gompa (prayer hall). The initiation was to take place at eight o'clock, so we took our places to wait for Rinpoche. He arrived at around nine and, after preliminary prayers, began by telling us about Tara and explaining the benefits of doing the different Tara practices. That night Rinpoche gave us some very precious teachings. Time passes very quickly when he teaches, and soon I realized that it was already two in the morning. I looked around me and noticed that the hall was now quite empty – many of those who originally assembled had left, unable to stay awake or bear the cold. I, too, was having difficulty staying awake. I tried not to get distracted, but my body was aching and my legs were stiff. It was hard sitting still and cross-legged on the cold floor, especially since it is deemed rude to stretch your legs and point them toward holy Buddha statues. I marveled at Rinpoche's ability to sit like a Buddha for so many hours, and was even more amazed at his ability to stay wide awake throughout the evening's program. I was thinking, "If I feel so sleepy and tired, it must be a thousand times more so for Rinpoche." But his kindness is infinite and he only ever has one thought: to speed up our path to enlightenment.

By the time Rinpoche gave the initiation that early morning there were only a handful of people left in the hall, of the original 200. It was karma, of course. When you are not ready, somehow a mundane thing like feeling sleepy is sufficient obstacle. But for those of us fortunate enough to have stayed on, Rinpoche was startlingly generous. He transmitted so many Tara practices that it really took our breath away. Today I have still to learn all the mantras and visualizations with which he empowered us during the initiation.

So from Rinpoche I learned that all the buddhas, with their different aspects and names, are born from the transcendental wisdom of great bliss; all the buddhas are manifestations of Dharmakaya. This is the meaning of "mother," the transcendental wisdom of non-dual bliss and voidness, which manifests in Tara. This purest consciousness manifests in the female aspect labeled "Tara, Mother of the Victorious Ones." This is not an easy concept to comprehend, but it is part of the wisdom that we meditate on to learn and understand.

You know, when there is some really serious pain or problem, somehow, naturally, even grown-ups call on their mother. However, Tara is much closer to you than a mother. Tara is called "mother" because it is the mother who gives birth to children. The meaning of Tara is the transcendental wisdom of great bliss, seeing the absolute truth and the conventional truth of all existence. This is the absolute guru – the actual, real guru. All the buddhas are born from this absolute guru, this transcendental wisdom of non-dual bliss and voidness. In reality, every buddha is the embodiment of this absolute guru, and the essence of all the buddhas is the absolute guru: one manifests in many; many manifest in one. The guru manifests in all these various aspects of Buddha. This is the real meaning of the guru; this is what you should think and understand.

LAMA KYABJE ZOPA RINPOCHE ON TARA AS
MOTHER-LIBERATOR

The benefits of Tara practice

Tara is the swift liberator – she is known for the speed with which she answers all supplications made to her. So she holds the key to quickly gaining the realizations that lead to the ultimate happiness of enlightenment. If you recite the Praises to the Twenty-One Taras with devotion, at dawn or dusk – or merely make a point to remember Tara daily, to sing her praises, and recite her mantras at any time of the day or night – this will protect you from fear and danger.

All your wishes, whatever they may be, will come true and you will receive extraordinary good fortune. Tara practice also saves you from the suffering rebirths of future lives. But the greatest benefit is that you will create the cause to receive initiations from many buddhas, which will eventually lead you to enlightenment and ultimate buddhahood.

Of more immediate concern to many and the temporal benefits from doing Tara practice. Tara helps you, with the swiftness of lightning, with problems that plague your day-to-day life; she intervenes to save you from untimely death; and she helps you recover from fatal illnesses. Tara also brings success in business and careers, and can help you find a job, bring you wealth, and overcome all obstacles. The extent of her blessing presence in your life is infinite, and impossible to enumerate.

Making a Tara statue – one of twenty-one – cast in bronze and gold. The gold is burnished with a jade-tipped tool.

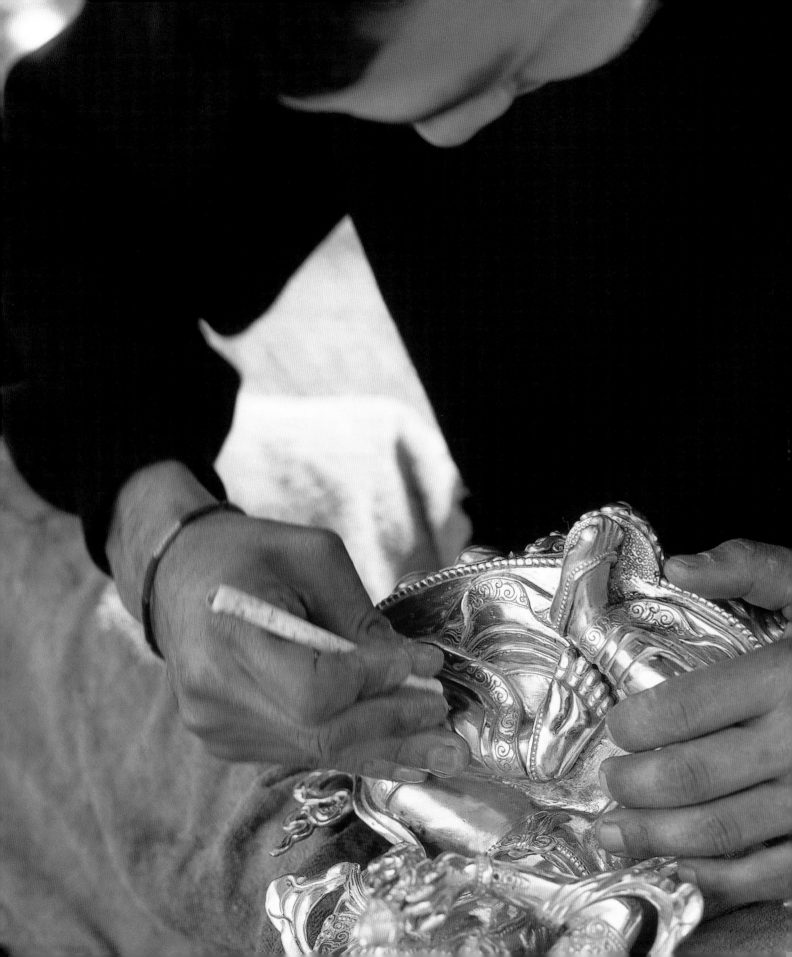

The visualization of Tara

Tara's mantra is recited as the goddess is visualized at the level of the forehead, and about one body's length away. The person visualizing thinks of the blissful wisdom of all the buddhas, fully seeing all existence, and of the holy Dharmakaya mind which is the absolute guru.

Tara manifests as extremely green light, with one face and two arms; she looks peaceful and has a sweet smile. Her hair is dark, half down and half tied up. In her hair is a blue utpala flower, and she is adorned with jewel ornaments.

Her eyes express the compassion and loving kindness that a mother gives her single, most-beloved child. Tara's right hand, holding the stem of an utpala flower, is in the mudra of granting sublime realization. Her left hand holds the stem of another utpala flower, with three fingers held upright to signify the Triple Gem – the Buddha, Dharma, and Sangha. Tara's right leg is stretched out, and the left one is folded. She sits on a moon disk and is adorned with the holy signs of a buddha.

At her forehead is a white Om, signifying the essence of her vajra holy body. White nectar beams are visualized coming from the Om, touching and penetrating the person's forehead. The beams purify all obstacles and negative karmas accumulated from beginningless time. The rays of white light cause immediate purification.

At Tara's throat is a red syllable Ah, the essence of her holy speech. From this, red nectar beams radiate; they touch the throat, instantly purifying all negative karmas caused by speech over a thousand lifetimes.

From Tara's heart and the blue syllable Hum, the essence of her holy mind, blue nectar beams radiate, entering a person's own heart. All obstacles and negative karmas caused by the impure thoughts of the mind and accumulated from beginningless rebirths are also purified.

One concentrates on this visualization, then recites at least one mala (108 repeats) of Tara's mantra: Om Tare Tuttare Ture Svaha.

The holy mind of all the buddhas is bound by compassion toward all beings, and so they manifest and take form as Tara. Her presence thus arises from her great compassion.

EIGHT OFFERINGS TO MOTHER TARA

A stunning eight-offering ritual to Tara is one of the most powerful practices, especially when undertaken while reciting appropriate mantras and making the accompanying mudra (see below). Making extensive offerings while reciting Tara mantras is highly recommended, but if time is short, the simple mandala offering ritual (see page 252) can be practiced.

Each offering is preceded by a mudra made by crossing the left wrist over the right in front of the breast, with the palms of both hands facing outward. One snaps his or her fingers simultaneously, then performs the mudra and chants the mantra of the offering in question. Immediately afterward, the same snapping gesture is made with the fingers, but this time with the right wrist crossed over the left.

1. **Water for drinking: Om Argham Ah Hum**
   The hands are held at breast level to form the likeness of a shallow bowl. Part of the rim consists of the thumbs resting on the gently curved fingers. As this hand gesture is made, the accompanying mantra is chanted.

2. **Water for bathing: Om Padyam Ah Hum**
   The left hand forms a fist, palm upward. The right hand is rotated, with fingers closed, from palm down to palm upward, unraveling the fingers as if water flows from the hand.

3. **Flowers: Om Pupe Ah Hum**
   The hands are placed back to back at breast level, with fingers interlaced and fingertips pointing upward. The tips of the index fingers touch, forming the shape of a flower bud, and the thumbs rest on the sides of the index fingers.

4. **Incense: Om Dhupe Ah Hum**
   With palms facing, the fingers are interlaced with index fingers extended parallel and thumbs extended upward, to suggest incense rising.

5. **Light: Om Aloke Ah Hum**

   At breast level the hands are held out, palms upward. Both hands make a fist, and both middle fingers are extended straight outward. The thumbs touch the middle joint of the middle fingers.

6. **Perfumed water: Om Gandhe Ah Hum**

   The left hand makes a fist, palm upward. The right hand is vertical, palm outward, with the thumb slightly curved. The right wrist rests on the edge of the left hand.

7. **Pure food: Om Niude Ah Hum**

   The hands form a bowl, exactly as for the first mudra, except that the thumbs are curled inward with the index fingers bent, to suggest a shallow bowl containing food.

8. **Music: Om Shabda Ah Hum**

   The thumbs hold down the ring and little fingers, then one extends the index and third fingers of each hand horizontally. The hands move alternately up and down, as if playing a drum.

When the offering ritual is complete, Tara's basic mantra can be recited, as well as either the Abbreviated Praise or the Praises to the Twenty-One Taras (see below). During the recitation, one imagines that from the body of Tara(s), a stream of nectar comes into their body and that all negativity is purged. Irrespective of which practice is performed, it is always a good idea to recite at least one mala of Tara's all-powerful basic mantra:

OM TARE TUTTARE TURE SVAHA

Even if this mantra is recited and nothing else is practiced, the mantra in itself is very powerful. There are Tara devotees who have recited her mantra a million times and tell me that they feel unutterably blessed. One can make any kind of commitment to do many thousands of mantras, although it is a good idea to consult your guru first.

Three different practices to Tara

These three inspiring Tara practices that can be combined or practiced individually: the Abbreviated Praise to Tara; the Practice of Tara's Promise; and Praises to the Twenty-One Taras.

White Tara in bronze decorated with lapis lazuli.

THE ABBREVIATED PRAISE TO TARA

This practice is easier and less time-consuming than the full Praises. Reciting it twenty-one times daily is said to bring incredible blessings:

OM CHOM DEN DAYMA
PHAG MO DROLMA LA
CHAGTSELO
CHAG TSAL DROLMA TARE PELMO
TUTTARA YI JIG KUN SELMA
TURE DUN NAM TAMCHAY TERMA
SVAHA YI GHE CHE LA RAB DU

Translation:

Om I prostrate to the exalted Goddess foe destroyer,
Liberating Mother Tara!
Homage to TARE, saviorness, heroine,
TUTTARE is dispelling all fears,
TURE is granting all the success
I respectfully bow to the letters SVAHA.

Green light and nectar is visualized, flowing from Mother Tara's heart and entering one's own body, speech, and mind. It purifies all the defilements caused with body, speech, and mind, and one receives the bliss of light and is absorbed into oneself, so one becomes one with Tara. This oneness is concentrated upon intensely. Then from the pores of one's own body, one imagines emitting light which purifies all sentient beings.

THE PRACTICE OF TARA'S PROMISE

Whenever someone has an urgent need or a special request to make – for instance, to pray for someone to recover from a serious illness, be successful in a job application, seek a reconciliation, or gain more blessings from their guru – this is a wonderful long mantra to recite. I have been advised that simply by remembering this mantra, all fears and dangers get dispelled and realizations will be achieved. One can make extensive offerings to Tara on the Tibetan eighth and fifteenth of each Tibetan lunar month, and then recite the mantra until one actually sees the goddess. Then whatever is wished for will be granted, as will all one's sublime realizations.

When there is a serious problem, such as some potentially

fatal disease, if you rely on Tara, it is a very common

experience that you will be liberated from that problem.

By doing Tara practice, you will recover from the disease.

If you eat poison and you rely on Tara, the poison will

not harm you.

TARA MANTRA FOR SUCCESS AND DISPELLING OBSTACLES

ARYA TARA SARWA PATI GYANA MA TARA NI

In the Tibetan language, this mantra is called "Promised by the Arya Mother Liberator Herself."

I prostrate to the Aryan Mother. Then recite the mantra

TAYA TA, OM TARA TARA YA, HUNH HUNG HUNG
SAMAR YAM TIDAI, BARA BARA
SARVA BARA NU
BIBU KITAI, PHE MANI PEMA, MAHA PEMA
ASANI TARTAI, HASA HASA,
TELOKA BARUDA, SARVA DEVA TARNA PHA,
PUZI DAI MARA HA,
BHARGARWARTA TARE, MARA HE,
BHARGARWAN, TATHAGATA SARYA, PURATA,
SAMAY YAM, TARA TARA, MAHA SARTVA,
AWALUKITAI, MA-NIKA NIKA, PITZI PHA BHA RA NEI
OM BEE LOKAR YA _____
(insert your name or names of patrons you are praying for)
BHARAWANTAI, TARA, SHRING SHRING SHRING
   PHE SOHA

Just remembering this mantra dispels all the fears and dangers. One will achieve all the realisations, and have control over all sentient beings. By making extensive offerings to Tara on the Tibetan 8th day and 15th day of each month and reciting this mantra until you actually see Tara, then whatever is wished for will be granted, and all sublime realizations will be granted. This incredibly precious practice comes from the Tantra of the Sublime Vajra, and it bestows inconceivable benefits.

PRAISES TO THE TWENTY-ONE TARAS

The version given here is based on Martin Wilson's marvelously chantable translation, and was checked against the Tibetan language by the staff of the Education Department of the FPMT. I have reproduced this version of the Praises simply because it is one of the most beautiful and powerful mantra prayers I have learned.

When you chant these praises, something magical happens and you feel yourself transcend into another realm and be carried aloft by the energy you create ... Go slowly initially, and feel the words and meanings transcending your consciousness. Soon you will discover your own rhythm. It is an excellent idea to offer three prostrations to Tara, the mother-liberator, before you begin. The word "homage" here actually means "I prostrate" (the Tibetan word for it is Chag Tsal). After each verse visualize Tara manifesting and dissolving into your heart.

Each of the twenty-one emanations of Tara is a different color and an entity in her own right, addressing different manifestations of our existence that require assistance from the goddess. There are also individual mantras to each of the Taras; however, these have not been reproduced here as they must be directly transmitted to you by a lineage lama. For easy visualization, look at a detailed painting of the twenty-one Taras (opposite and overleaf) and keep it in your mind as you recite the Praises. Remember mentally to make prostrations as you think of each of the emanations.

Right and overleaf: Thangka
paintings depicting the
Twenty-one Taras.

A DESCRIPTION OF THE TWENTY-ONE TARAS

1. Red Tara, the quick heroine who grants the power of control and effective persuasion
2. The great peaceful White Tara, who pacifies spirit harms, negative karma, delusions, and diseases
3. The great increasing one, Golden Tara, who increases life, merit, good fortune, wealth, and fame
4. The great long-life Yellow Tara, who grants longevity
5. The great Hum-making Orange Tara, who brings other beings close to you
6. Black-Red Tara, victorious over the Three Worlds, who protects you from spirit harm by making the spirits crazy
7. Black Tara, slightly wrathful, who dispels all black magic and harmful spells
8. Red Tara, destroyer of the enemy Mara, who destroys the four types of mara
9. White Tara, the three sublime, who protects all beings from fear and danger
10. Red Tara, destroyer of maras, who controls the world
11. Orange Tara, eliminator of poverty, who brings wealth
12. The Orange Tara of auspicious beauty, who makes everything auspicious
13. Fire-blazing Red Tara, who pierces your enemy but does not harm others*
14. Black Tara, slightly wrinkled and wrathful, who pierces interference
15. White Tara, the great pacifier, who brings harmony
16. Red Tara, liberating with wisdom-Hum, for wisdom and increasing the power of mantras
17. Orange Tara, shaking the three worlds, who controls the power of mantras
18. White Tara, who eliminates poisons and overcomes their effects
19. White Tara, for release from prison and overcoming quarrels and fights
20. Orange Tara, for eliminating contagious diseases
21. White Tara, whose venerable actions make all activities successful.

* the real enemy is the delusion of one's own mind

Here are the Praises to the Twenty-One Taras:

Let me and all who need protection,
Enter beneath your right-hand mudra
Of granting boons and refuge mudra,
And be relieved from every fear.

Om! I prostrate to the noble transcendent liberator.

1. Homage! Tara, swift, heroic!
Eyes like lightning instantaneous!
Sprung from op'ning stamens of the
Lord of Three Worlds' tear-born lotus!

2. Homage! She whose face combines a
Hundred autumn moons at fullest!
Blazing with light-rays resplendent,
As a thousand-star collection!

3. Homage! Golden- blue one lotus,
Water-born, in hand adorned!
Giving, effort, calm, austerities,
Patience, meditation her sphere!

4. Homage! Crown of tathagatas,
Actions triumph without limit!
Relied on by conqueror's children,
Having reached ev'ry perfection!

5. Homage! Filling with Tuttara,
Hum, desire, direction, and space!
Trampling with her feet the seven worlds,
Able to draw forth all beings!

6. Homage! Worshipped by the all-lords,
Sakra, Agni, Brahma, Marut!
Honored by the hosts of spirits,
Corpse-raisers, gandhavars, yakshas!

7. Homage! with Her Trad and Phat sounds
Destroying foes' magic diagrams!
Her feet pressing, left out, right in,
Blazing in a raging fire-blaze!

8. Homage! Ture, very dreadful!
Destroyer of Mara's champion(s)!
She with frowning lotus visage
Who is slayer of all enemies!

9. Homage! At her heart her fingers
Adorn her with Three Jewel mudra!
Light-ray masses all excited!
All directions' wheels adorn her!

10. Homage! She so joyous, radiant,
Crown emitting garlands of light!
Mirthful, laughing with Tuttare,
Subjugating maras, devas!

11. Homage! She able to summon
All earth-guardians' assembly!
Shaking, frowning, with her Hum sign
Saving from every misfortune!

12. Homage! Crown adorned with crescent
Moon, all ornaments most shining!
Amitabha in her hair-knot
Sending out much light eternal!

13. Homage! She 'mid wreath ablaze like
Eon-ending fire abiding!
Right stretched, left bent, joy surrounds you
Troops of enemies destroying!

14. Homage! She who strikes the ground with
Her palm, and with her foot beats it!
Scowling, with the letter Hum
the Seven levels she does conquer!

15. Homage! Happy, virtuous, peaceful!
She whose field is peace, nirvana!
She endowed with Om and Svaha,
Destroyer of the great evil!

16. Homage! She with joy surrounded
Tearing foes' bodies asunder
Frees with Hum and knowledge mantra,
Arrangement of the ten letters!

17. Homage! Ture! With seed letter
Of the shape of syllable Hum
By foot stamping shakes the three worlds,
Meru, Mandara, and Vindhya!

18. Homage! Holding in her hand the
Deer-marked moon of deva- lake form!
With twice-spoken Tara and Phat,
Totally dispelling poison!

19. Homage! She whom Gods and their kings,
and the kinnaras do honor!
Armored in all joyful splendor,
She dispels bad dreams and conflicts!

20. Homage! She whose eyes bright with
Radiance of sun and full moon!
With twice Hara and Tuttara
She dispels severe contagion!

21. Homage! Full of liberating
Pow'r by set of three natures!
Destroys hosts of spirits, yakshas,
And raised corpses! Supreme! Ture!
These praises with the root mantras
And prostrations thus are twenty-one!

The following dedications may be made:

Due to the vast merit I create with this practice, please,
mother Tara, may I soon attain your enlightened state that I
may liberate all sentient beings from their suffering. May the
precious bodhi mind in me, not yet born, arise and grow.
May the bodhichitta already born within me have no decline
but instead increase for evermore.

In all my rebirths may I never be separated from perfect
spiritual masters and enjoy the magnificent Dharma. May
I complete all qualities and stages of the path and may I
quickly attain the state of Vajradhara.

8

Chenrezig, the Buddha of Compassion, manifests as Jambhala to grant wealth to relieve the poverty of all sentient beings.

LAMA KYABJE ZOPA RINPOCHE

Meeting the Wealth Buddhas

The legend of Jambhala

The legend of Jambhala, the Tibetan wealth-giving buddha, goes back to the time of Lama Atisha in the eleventh century. It is said that one day Lama Atisha was walking near Bodhgaya when he saw an old man dying of starvation. Moved by his suffering, the lama wanted to cut his own flesh to offer the old man, who shook his head, saying, "How can I eat a monk's flesh?" Atisha thought, "Of course, he cannot. But how can I stand to see him suffering?" Then the lama lay down, feeling helpless and sad, and wondering what he could do. Suddenly a white light appeared and, looking up, Lama Atisha saw 1,000-armed Chenrezig, the Buddha of Compassion, who said to Atisha, "I will manifest as Jambhala, the Buddha of Wealth, to help others by eliminating their poverty, making it possible for them to practice the Dharma."

Chenrezig, the Compassion Buddha, therefore came to manifest as the wealth-giving Buddha, whose name is Jambhala (also spelt Dzambhala). The Indian origins of Jambhala are reflected in his appearance. Over time not one but five wealth Jambhalas have evolved, each with his own mantra and practices, which can help in the elimination of poverty and in attracting financial stability to enable you to practice the spiritual path. Of the five, I am most familiar with the practice of the White and Yellow Jambhalas, both of which I received through the kindness of my guru. I have also been fortunate enough to receive initiation to the White Jambhala practice from Rinpoche.

Yellow Jambhala, one of the principal bestowers of wealth, with Shakyamuni Buddha (top center), White Tara (bottom left) and Green Tara (bottom right).

The Five Jambhalas for Abundance

The Yellow Jambhala sits on a lotus, sun, and moon disk and holds a mongoose in his left hand, from whose mouth spew forth precious jewels. The White Jambhala sits on a turquoise dragon and his left hand holds a mongoose, which also spits out precious diamonds and ornaments. I have included their two practices – to the White and Yellow Jambhalas – later in this chapter.

The other three Jambhalas are the Black Jambhala, who is usually depicted standing, with a wrathful expression, surrounded by a ring of fire; the Green Jambhala, who is usually shown in a tight embrace with his consort; and the Red Jambhala, who is sometimes shown with the head of an elephant. Some say that the Red Jambhala is the Hindu god of wealth, the stunningly popular Lord Ganesh. All the Jambhalas generally carry the jewel-spouting mongoose in their left hand, which helps wealth to flow into your home when you do the Jambhala practice with sincere motivation.

As everyone knows, when there are enough funds, it is easier for the mind to practice the unselfish way of thinking and to develop an attitude of generosity to others. So the purpose of practicing Jambhala is to eliminate the insecurity of worrying about money, so that you are not distracted by hunger, poverty, or lack of funds. Many people worry about where the next meal is coming from, and this represents a great distraction on the spiritual path. The Jambhala practice helps dissolve the karma of poverty. It is also excellent for helping the monastic community (the Sangha) make it possible for people to become financially stable.

There are different ritualistic practices to invoke the help of the Jambhalas. These are not widely known, and not many lamas hold the lineage that enables them to give initiation or oral transmissions of the Jambhalas' mantras and rituals. I have learned how to make the White Jambhala wealth vase, because it is very similar to the Chinese concept of making wealth vases to enhance the feng shui of a family home. Jambhala wealth vases have to be consecrated and kept hidden from view. The ritual of consecration requires someone who is well versed in the practice and has received initiation from a lineage lama. The consecration of a wealth vase involves making extensive offerings and chanting many thousands of mantras.

Red Jambhala is associated with the Hindu elephant-god, Ganesh. Boudhanath Stupa, Nepal, has this shrine to Ganesh at its entrance.

Water offerings to the Jambhalas

The other beneficial practice is making daily water offerings to the Jambhalas, which requires the simultaneous recitation of mantras. This can be done for the White, Yellow, and Black Jambhalas at one session or for each individually. The ritual requires water offerings to be made on the heads of the Jambhalas (or, in the case of the Black Jambhala, onto the stomach).

The Venerable Ribur Rinpoche once explained that when Devadatta – Shakyamuni Buddha's cousin, who was jealous of him – threw rocks at the Buddha to harm him, the Jambhalas came around the Buddha. The rocks hit the White and Yellow Jambhalas on their heads and the Black Jambhala on the stomach. This is why the first two Jambhalas feel bliss when a water offering is poured on their head – it eases their hurt. For the same reason, water should be poured on the stomach of the Black Jambhala. In return, the Jambhalas grant prosperity.

Rinpoche also says that it is beneficial to use the offering water to practice generosity to the wretched creatures known as pretas from the realm of the hungry ghosts, who are able to quench their terrible thirst by tasting the water that has flowed down the Jambhala's body. This act of generosity will add to the practitioner's merit, thereby strengthening the Jambhala practice.

As always, any spiritual practice should begin with a strong motivation, by first taking refuge, generating bodhichitta, and thinking through the Four Immeasurable Thoughts (see page 23). The aspiration should be not simply to get rich by doing the Jambhala practice, but to get rich in order to practice generosity and follow the spiritual path of wanting to benefit all other beings. One thinks, "The purpose of my life is to liberate all sentient beings from their sufferings and cause them to become enlightened, and for this I must achieve perfect buddhahood." To make the practice stronger, an idea of each realm's sufferings and experiences is imagined. It is excellent for a person to think of people who are suffering and of whom they are personally aware, because this makes their compassion more real, strong, and therefore more powerful. One thinks, "I must achieve enlightenment in order to help all suffering beings. Therefore I am going to make water offerings to Jambhala and make water charity to the pretas." This describes the two parts of the ritual.

Lama Kyabje Zopa Rinpoche advises doing the water offering ritual before lunch on an empty stomach, and to wash one's hands in preparation – otherwise the pretas are frightened by the smell of food on the hands.

WATER OFFERING TO THE WHITE JAMBHALA

I offer this water to the holy body of Jambhala, who is riding on the dragon. His body is white in color. His right hand is holding a trident, and his left hand has a club. He is encircled by the four dakinis*, one in each of the cardinal directions.

One thinks the above as water is offered onto the Jambhala's head. As the water is poured with the right hand, he fingers of the left hand are snapped in front of the heart (as a reminder of the wisdom of emptiness) and the mantra is recited.

OM PADMA KRODA ARYA JAMBHALA HRI DAYA HUM PHET

This is recited seven or twenty-one times (or as many times as possible). The most important thing is to visualize the Jambhala as the root guru. One imagines that from the mouth of the dragon (and from the mongoose, if he holds one) – like beautiful water cascading down from the mountains – come lots of wish-fulfilling jewels, or billions and billions of dollars. The water generates great bliss on the head of the Jambhala. After receiving the water, the Jambhala's mind is so inspired that he promises to help bring all that is needed for a project, for a company's profits, for improvement in cash flow, and for all the attainments that have been wished for.

The Jambhalas at Kopan monastery, Nepal, live in a constant flow of water. For individual water offerings, it is best to use Jambhala statues that have been filled with mantras and properly consecrated. Water can then be poured over them, and their appropriate mantras recited.

* fairy maidens or goddesses

WATER OFFERING TO THE YELLOW JAMBHALA

One visualizes that the seed-syllable Jam transforms into the Yellow Jambhala and thinks:

By offering to the holy body water which cleans, all pains are pacified, Jambhala becomes fully sat-
isfied and experiences great bliss. Please, Jambhala, please grant all attainments and all the needs
requested.

Water is offered onto the Jambhala's head. As it is poured with the right hand, the fingers of the left are snapped in front of the heart. This mantra is recited as many times as possible:

OM JAMBHALA JALANDRAYE SVAHA

WATER OFFERING TO THE BLACK JAMBHALA

The mantra is recited seven or twenty-one times, while performing the same actions as before, but pouring water onto the Jambhala's stomach.

OM JLUM SOHA
OM INDRAYANI MUKHAM BHRAMARI SOHA

To conclude the ritual, fervent request prayers are made. Then, using the fingers, water is flicked to the center and to the four directions, signifying that the poverty of all sentient beings in the ten directions is eliminated. Then the fingers are dipped in a little water and tasted in order to receive the attainment. As this is being done, this mantra is recited:

JAMBHALA SIDDHI PHA LA HO

Yellow Jambhala sits on a
lotus before a moon disk.
In his left hand he holds a
mongoose.

Making water charity to the pretas

Rinpoche says that, according to what he learned from his own guru, the merit obtained from making charity to just one preta, or hungry ghost, is greater than that obtained from making charity to all sentient beings of the three lower realms.

If charity is made to one preta with flames coming out of his mouth, then more merit is collected than by making charity to the rest of the hungry ghosts, because the preta with flames coming out of his mouth has more suffering than the others. However, the preta who has two or three knots at his neck has even more suffering than the preta with flames coming out of his mouth. Therefore if water charity is made to the pretas with knots at the neck, greater merit is being collected than by making water charity to all the pretas with flames coming out of their mouths. The pretas with knots can get only a drop of water. When a person makes water charity, the knots are loosened and these pretas can drink the water. This purifies their mind and they get liberated from the lower realms. This practice is unbelievably beneficial.

In order to make water charity, a person visualizes himself or herself as Chenrezig, the Compassion Buddha, and imagines that his blessings are helping them to make the offering. They visualize that in their right hand is the seed-syllable HRIH, from which light beams emanate. Nectar flows through the beams and becomes a water offering to all the pretas. They are totally satisfied – the water purifies them of their negative karma and defilements.

Then, holding a container of water, water is poured with the mudra of supreme offering. (Open pots cannot be used, because if the pretas see an empty pot, they experience immense suffering and disappointment, so all water containers should have a lid.) The fingers of the left hand are snapped in front of the heart, in the mudra of granting refuge. Then this mantra is recited seven or twenty-one times: Om Ah Hrih Hum. This is water charity for general pretas.

Next, water charity is made to the pretas with flames coming out of their mouths. The mantra Om Mani Padme Hum is recited as many times as possible (but at least seven or twenty-one times). For these pretas, water is dropped outside the container.

Water charity is then made to the pretas with knots at their necks. This mantra is recited as many times as possible: Om Jvala Midam Sarwa Preta Jah Soha. The right hand is cupped and some water is poured outside the container, at the same time snapping the fingers of the left hand.

WIDENING THE PRACTICE

Rinpoche says that the following water offering can be made at a swimming pool, in the ocean, in a pond, river, lake, or any other large body of water to multiply the effect. I have accompanied him on several occasions when he was doing his daily morning charity practice.

A water-filled container is held up with the right hand, and the following mantra is recited seven times:

OM NYANA AWALOKITE SAMANTA SPARANA RASMI
BAWA SAMAYA MAHA MANI DURU DURU HRIDAYA
JALANI SOHA

The water is then poured into the pool, ocean, or river. The whole practice should be repeated seven times. In this way, all the water, like the Buddha's omniscient mind, appears as uncontaminated nectar to the pretas, who get liberated from the lower realms and reborn into a higher realm.

One blows on the water before it is poured into the larger body of water. The first time, the mantra Om Nyana Awalokite ... is chanted seven times, followed by Om Mani Padme Hum as often as possible. For the next six repeats, the mantra can be changed, and other powerful mantras inserted, such as the Medicine Buddha's mantra (see page 92), repeated at least seven times; White Tara's mantra (see page 163), repeated seven times; and Buddha Mitrugpa's mantra (see page 47), repeated seven times; and so on.

At least one of the powerful mantras for purification should be recited (see page 72), before pouring the water into the ocean. In this way, since the water is blessed when it mixes with the ocean, all the sentient beings in the ocean will be purified, helping them to attain a good rebirth. After the water has been poured, it is visualized as appearing as nectar to all the pretas that Buddha sees. The blessed water purifies their karmas and liberates them from suffering – they all become Chenrezig. Then dedications are made for the merit that has been created by doing this practice.

The White Jambhala daily practice

This is an abbreviated water offering to the Jambhala deities. One thinks:

For the purpose of keeping my morality pure, I am practicing to the wealth-giving protector of morality called the White Jambhala, who rides on a turquoise dragon. I am offering flowing water to the holy body. I pledge to make charity toward other sentient beings. Please grant me realizations.

First, heartfelt refuge is taken in the Triple Gem, which generates the bodhichitta mind of enlightenment in the heart. Then strong requests are made to the White Jambhala, who rides a turquoise dragon, sits on a lotus and moon disk, and carries a white trident and banner staff. He is surrounded by the four dakinis of the four cardinal directions.

An image or statue of the White Jambhala and his four dakinis can be arranged in a clean basin that is large enough to hold all the water to be offered. The Jambhala is placed in the center; the dakini holding a vajra in her upraised hand in front of him; the dakini holding a jewel on his right-hand side; the dakini holding a double vajra on his left-hand side; and the dakini holding a lotus behind him. The dakinis are all placed facing the central Jambhala. The water must be poured correctly: very slowly and continuously, in a gentle stream, over the dragon-riding Jambhala and the four dakinis, as the mantras are recited.

Lama Kyabje Zopa Rinpoche translated and dictated this practice to one of his Western monks, the Venerable Paul LeMay. He dedicated the merit gained to experiencing miraculous success – surpassing what the practitioner expects or can visualize.

WHITE JAMBHALA'S MANTRA

OM ARYA JAMBHALA ARGHAM PADJAM
PUPE DHUPE ALOKE GANDHE
NIEUDE SHABDA PRATITSA SVAHA

THE MANTRAS OF THE FOUR DAKINIS

OM VAJRA DAKINI HUM PHET
OM RATNA DAKINI HUM PHET
OM PADMA DAKINI HUM PHET
OM KARMA DAKINI HUM PHET

Lama Kyabje Zopa Rinpoche advises reciting the mantras a hundred times – or 1,000 times, in periods of great need or serious financial crisis. Visualized from the holy mouth of the White Jambhala and the dragon are hundreds of millions of dollars, wish-fulfilling jewels, and so on, like a waterfall cascading unceasingly from the mountains. These are granted, and they fill one's family house, monastery, or Dharma center. The mantra Sarva Siddhi Hum is recited. Forgiveness is requested by reciting to the White Jambhala:

> *Please have patience with any mistakes I have made by not having completely understood, being unable to do the practice correctly and completely, and so forth.*

For purification, the hundred-syllable Vajrasattva mantra is recited (see page 72). Eight offerings are made with this offering mantra:

OM PEMA KRODHA ARYA JAMBHALA SAPARIWARA
(ARGHAM / PADYAM / PUPE / DHUPE / ALOKE /
GANDHE / NIUDE SHABDA*)
PRATITSA HUM SOHA

* Each offering word is used in turn when the mantra is recited.

THE EIGHT WATER-BOWL OFFERINGS

1. Argham – drinking water
2. Padyam – water for bathing
3. Pupe – a flower offering
4. Dhupe – a light offering for the "holy eye" sense
5. Aloke – incense for the "holy nose" sense
6. Gandhe – scented water to sprinkle on the heart and "holy body"
7. Niude – an eating offering for the "holy mouth"
8. Shabda – a music offering for the "holy ear" sense.

The mantra can be recited eight times, filling in the appropriate word for each offering, accompanied by the hand mudras that go with them. Alternatively, the mantra is recited while visualizing the offering vividly. Next, the specially translated verse of praise is read (shown overleaf), then the merits of the practice are dedicated.

To the One who controls
harm-givers, whose holy body
is elegant in nine ways of
acting, who is well-tied with
rainbow aggregates made of
melted white crystal, who
grants wish-giving realizations
like a rainfall, I prostrate to
you, glorious Jambhala.

The Yellow Jambhala daily practice

Below is an abbreviated water offering to the Yellow Jambhala. One thinks:

NAMO GURUBHYE!

I take refuge in the guru Triple Gem: the Buddha, Dharma, and Sangha.

On a lotus and moon seat, from the syllable Jam, comes the Yellow Jambhala. He is visualized holding the fruit of total victory in his right hand and a mongoose in his left. He is adorned with silks, jewels, and garlands of flowers. To offer purification to his crown with flowing water bestows continual realizations. The mantra of the Yellow Jambhala, Om Jambhala Jalandraye Svaha, is recited while performing the water offering to the Jambhala's head. A thick stream of water can be offered if there is little time, but when there is time, a fine stream of water should be offered. The water is poured with the right hand, the fingers of the left hand are snapped in front of the heart, as a reminder of the wisdom of emptiness. The mantra is recited at least seven times (although doing a full mala is more beneficial). There is great merit in visualizing the Jambhala as one's root guru.

Yellow Jambhala with the five Tantric, or Dhanyi Buddhas.

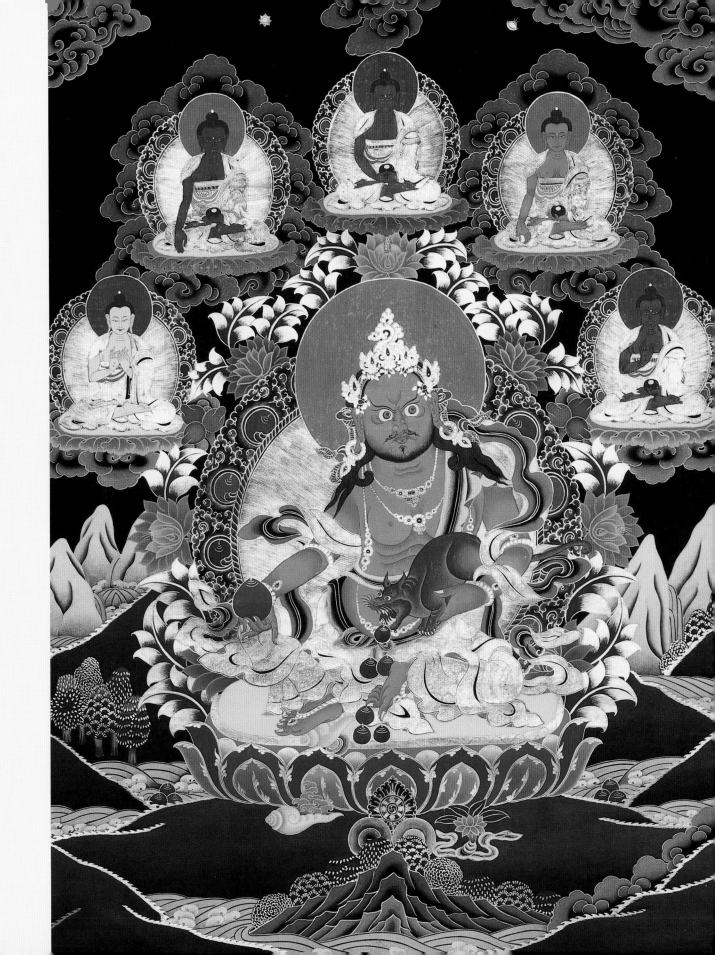

Like beautiful water cascading from the mountains, a torrent of wish-fulfilling jewels and billions of dollars are visualized falling from the mouth of the mongoose. The water flowing on the head of the Yellow Jambhala generates great bliss and his mind is deeply inspired. He promises to bring the financial success that is needed for any project.

At the end of the practice, this mantra is recited:

OM ARYA JAMBHALA ARGHAM SHABDA
PRATITSA SVAHA

Then one prays silently and fervently to the Yellow Jambhala:

> *Having obtained the power of concentration, you eliminate the poverty of beings. Wish-granting, jewel-like deity, I praise you with respect. Offering clean, fresh water completely pacifies suffering and bestows abundantly the realizations of food, clothing, wealth, and grain.*

In conclusion, a drop of the offering water is put onto the tongue; this water grants realizations that will ultimately lead to enlightenment. The following mantra is recited:

JAMBHALA SIDDHI PHALA HO

DEDICATIONS

When doing Jambhala practice it is important to take note of the special dedications to be included at the end of the practice, which are meditated upon:

> *Due to the merits three times accumulated by you, the buddhas and bodhisattvas, and all sentient beings, may the bodhichitta that is the source of all happiness and the success of myself and others be generated in your mind and in the minds of others without delay, even for a second. And where bodhichitta has already generated, may it increase.*

The merits are dedicated, in that any wealth received may be highly beneficial for Dharma centers, to complete extensive work on the teachings of Buddha, and for migrator beings or for oneself, one's family, or any acquaintance, to achieve success without encountering obstacles. The merits are dedicated in that the wealth received should never become the cause of samsara or rebirth into the lower realms – it should only become a cause of enlightenment:

> *Due to all the past, present, and future merits accumulated by me and all buddhas, bodhisattvas, and sentient beings, which are empty from their own side, may I, who am empty from my own side, achieve the Compassion Buddha's enlightenment, which is empty from its own side, and lead by myself all sentient beings, who are empty from their own side, to that enlightened state as quickly as possible.*

9

The great Maitreya will appear in this world

and achieve the great enlightenment.

LAMA CHOBGYE RINPOCHE

Meeting Maitreya,
the Buddha of the Future

THE MANTRA OF MAITREYA

NAMO RATNA TRAYA YA
NAMO BHAGAWATE SHAKYAMUNIYE
TATAGATAYA
ARHATE SAMYAKSAM BUDDHAYA
TAYATA
OM AJITE AJITE APARAJITE
AJITEN CHAYA
 HA RA HA RA MAITRI AWALOK ITE
KARA KARA MAHA SAMAYA SIDDHI
BHARA BHARA MAHA BODHI MENDA BIJA
MARA MARA EMA KAM SAMAYA
BODHI BODHI MAHA BODHI SOHA
OM MOHI MOHI MAHA MOHI SOHA
OM MUNI MUNI MARA SOHA

Maitreya Buddha is usually shown seated on a throne supported by eight snow lions, and he is about to rise in response to the needs of a degenerate world. On his head is a stupa, symbolizing respect for Shakyamuni Buddha. Above his head is a parasol, one of the eight auspicious objects, signifying Maitreya's powers of protection against evil influences.

Building the Buddha of Love

Maitreya is the Buddha of the future, the fifth teaching Buddha in this eon of 1,000 Buddhas. One day soon a magnificent bronze statue of the future Buddha Maitreya – a statue three times larger than the Statue of Liberty – will arise on the holy ground of Bodhgaya in India. This is the site of Shakyamuni Buddha's enlightenment under the bodhi tree and the holiest place of pilgrimage for Buddhists of all traditions. The Maitreya statue will be a unique feat of timeless beauty and modern engineering and will be built to stand for 1,000 years, sending forth its universal message of loving kindness.

The idea of building a gigantic statue of the future Buddha in Bodhgaya took seed in the mind of the twentieth-century yogi Lama Thubten Yeshe. With his disciple, Lama Kyabje Zopa Rinpoche, Lama Yeshe was among the many high lamas who fled Tibet when the Dalai Lama left in 1959. At first they lived in the refugee camps given to them by a sympathetic India. Then they began teaching the words and wisdom of Buddha to the world. Together, Lama Yeshe and Lama Zopa established the FPMT, which over the years expanded into a worldwide network of meditation centers, monasteries, nunneries, hospices, and schools, all dedicated to making available the Mahayana teachings of the Buddha. Lama Yeshe has since passed on and reincarnated as a Spanish boy born in 1985 who is currently seventeen years old, Lama Osel Rinpoche. He presently resides at Sera monastery in southern India, preparing for the time when he will carry on the work started during his previous incarnation.

In the meantime Lama Kyabje Zopa Rinpoche guides the spiritual programs of the FPMT centers, monasteries, hospices, and schools. He has made it his life's work to transform his heart-guru's seed-idea of a Maitreya statue into reality. At the time of writing, land has been purchased to house the statue; a computer-simulated enlargement of the prototype has been completed; and detailed designs have been finalized to ensure that the statue will endure. It will be the largest holy object in the world – and, according to the sacred scriptures, everyone associated with the project will benefit from eventual rebirth as a direct disciple of Maitreya, thereby gaining enlightenment for the sake of all beings. This is the promise of Maitreya. The project is ongoing, and anyone who wishes to be involved in its actualization can contact the management team at the address given on page 268.

Maitreya Buddha's hands are in the teaching mudra, holding the stems of lotuses, on which are the Dharma wheel and a vase.

The practice of Maitreya Buddha

My very first experience of a puja came in Bodhgaya in February 1997, when I met Lama Kyabje Zopa Rinpoche. I had accepted his invitation to Bodhgaya, intrigued by the prospect of making the first pilgrimage of my life. So I flew to India and endured the journey to Bodhgaya – by plane from Delhi to Patna, and then by four-hour car ride to Gaya, on rough roads, passing dried-out river beds and dusty villages before reaching Bodhgaya itself. I had envisaged the worst, having heard about the numbing poverty of Bodhgaya, the beggars, the dust, and the dirt, and all of these scenes played out before my eyes. But, strangely, one never forgets how immensely holy the place is.

You can feel it in the air – a special something that embraces your heart and mind, so that all judgmental thoughts seem to stay frozen, even as you stand in awe at the entrance to the tiny shrine room where the most magnificent image of the Buddha gazes serenely at you. I recall those few days as in a dream, and that first puja – an offering prayer ritual, not unlike a mass.

My guide on that first visit was the Venerable Marcel, a tall, good-looking Dutchman who had been a monk for nearly twenty-three years. Marcel speaks English and has been a devoted disciple, first of Lama Yeshe and then of Lama Zopa, for a very long time. At the time of my visit Marcel was director of the Maitreya statue project, so it was he who came to meet me at Delhi airport and brought me to Bodhgaya. During our second afternoon there, after Lama Kyabje Zopa Rinpoche had also arrived, he asked if I wanted to attend that evening's puja – when 1,000 light offerings were to be made to Maitreya. The puja was to be led by Rinpoche and held under the bodhi tree – the same tree under which the Buddha had attained enlightenment.

"We start at eight," he said to me. "And eat before you come, for it could be quite late by the time we finish." I did not heed his advice. I felt confident I could hold off the hunger pangs, even if we finished at midnight. That was foolishness on my part, but since meeting the buddhas I have come to realize that I have been living life rather foolishly. Slowly I find myself learning many things to which I was previously blind.

That evening we all gathered under the bodhi tree. Lama Zopa was already there. The 1,000 candles and other offerings – 1,000 bowls of water, 1,000 vases filled with flowers, 1,000 food offerings, and 1,000 incense sticks – made for a mountain of offerings. I wondered when they had arranged them all.

There were mats to allow us to sit on the dirt ground, prayer books to enable us to follow the puja, and torch lights to read by in the dark. There were so many monks and nuns – where did they all come from, I wondered? Most impressive of all was the "throne" on which Lama Kyabje Zopa Rinpoche sat. It was a beautiful makeshift throne, covered with elaborately embroidered brocade and cushions.

But it was all very intimidating, because everyone seemed to know what to do, what prayers to say, what rituals to follow. I felt rather foolish as I saw them do their prostrations on the cold, hard earth, mumbling their mantras and getting very quickly into the mood of the puja. I was feeling rather out of it and my mind was wandering, so I made myself very small, closed my eyes, and hoped that Maitreya Buddha would forgive me for being so unfamiliar with the rituals. I remember thinking that all this ritual stuff was perhaps not for me. Later when I asked Lama Zopa why there were so many rituals and his answer came, "What is wrong with rituals, when there is so much meaning to them?"

Incense made by nuns at Kopan monastery uses the purest herbs gathered from the Himalayan region.

Indeed, but that evening it was hard for me to focus my mind and concentrate. All that was happening was new to me. As if hearing my unspoken thoughts, Lama Kyabje Zopa Rinpoche turned to look at me and must have said something, because soon I felt someone passing to me the puja book turned to exactly the right page. Merry Colony is one of Rinpoche's oldest disciples and is very beautiful, blonde, and smiling. She gave me a very warm smile as she used her finger to point to the words, and passed me a torch so that I could read in the dark.

You will discover that when you can follow what is going on, it is easier to get into the spirit of things and enjoy the puja. We moved from page to page, following Marcel as he led the chanting of the offering mantras and other preliminary prayers. And so we recited, and time seemed to stand still. We must have been going on for about two hours when I started to feel the cold. I shuddered, wishing I had brought a shawl. No one had warned me that the temperature in Bodhgaya drops massively when night falls.

And then there were the mosquitoes – swarms of them … I could hear them in my ear distracting me, making me miserable and wonder when the puja would finish. I was also beginning to feel hungry. Then I thought, "It's easy for Lama Kyabje Zopa Rinpoche and all the monks and nuns, for they have their robes to keep them warm, and to stop the mosquitoes from biting them."

Something made me glance toward Rinpoche and I felt the color rush to my face as I saw his bare arms exposed. It appeared that he had shrugged off his robes on purpose. I saw so many mosquitoes feeding on his exposed arms that it made me draw my breath in shame. Instantly I stop warding off the mosquitoes. Later I was told that Rinpoche does this all the time when there is an opportunity – making an offering to the mosquitoes of his blood. When I asked him about it, he laughed as if in rejoicing. "Only one drop of blood," I recall him telling me. It seemed churlish to talk about the diseases carried by mosquitoes …

Rinpoche also did not seem to mind the cold. As I had these thoughts, he turned around to look at me again. Something inside me wanted to please him, so I made myself get into the spirit of the puja. Instinctively I knew that this is what he would want me to do: enjoy the ritual. Rinpoche's encouraging glance must have given me the inspiration to carry on for another hour or so.

By then I realized that we had finished the long preliminaries and had started reciting the Maitreya Buddha mantra – I only realized it was a mantra when I discerned everyone reciting it over and over again. We kept going back to page 49, where the mantras began, and then it seemed as if the rest of the night was spent going back to that page. Again and again, so that soon I began to transcend into a sort of trance, as the words and syllables of the mantra took on familiarity. The mantra of the Maitreya Buddha is long, and the syllables take time to get used to, but once they penetrate the mind, the mantra creates its own magic. Soon I found myself drifting, feeling unaccountably happy. I had stopped turning the pages, for I had learned the mantra through all those repetitions. Later I was told that that night Rinpoche said that we were to recite the mantra 100,000 times. So by the time we finished the puja, it was already the early hours of the morning – around five o'clock. And so the Maitreya mantra, reproduced on page 228, was the first one that I received as an oral transmission from Lama Kyabje Zopa Rinpoche.

Developing compassion helps us develop wisdom, especially the wisdom that realizes emptiness, the ultimate nature of the I, the mind and all other phenomena. This wisdom gradually thins the clouds of obscurations that temporarily obscure the mind until the mind becomes as pure as clear blue sky flooded with sunlight.

LAMA KYABJE ZOPA RINPOCHE

Overleaf: Evening puja at Kopan monastery, lead by Lama Lhundrup Khen Rinpoche.

Chobgye Rinpoche's revelation

Ayear before the 1,000-light-offering puja to Maitreya, the Venerable Marcel's people had organized another kind of puja, a bhumi puja, on the land where the statue of Maitreya is to be built. That puja was to bless the land, and one of Rinpoche's oldest gurus, the Venerable Chobgye Trichen Rinpoche, attended in a wheelchair. It was a special occasion, when he offered the most valuable background to the cosmic king and his 1,000 sons, who all become buddhas.

Chobgye Trichen Rinpoche is an authentic old-style lama from Tibet, where all things learned from the sutras are committed to memory. So his explanation of the Buddhas of our age was very precious. What I reproduce here are lightly edited extracts from a transcript of Chobgye Rinpoche's amazing revelation that night. It belongs to the FPMT, which has a precious collection of transcripts comprising every word ever spoken at any teaching by Rinpoche and his gurus.

[Lama Kyabje Zopa] Rinpoche has asked me to say something about the benefits and qualities of Maitreya Buddha. In 1959, the Chinese takeover of Tibet was a great blow to Buddhism, which is the sole light of the entire world. But great determination was generated in the mind of His Holiness the Dalai Lama who, with many of his followers, came to India, and His Holiness has preserved and promoted the dying culture of Tibet, and especially Buddhism, all over the world …

Now to relate about the formation of the world.

It takes so many eons to form the planets, of which there are infinite numbers. Among these infinite worlds there are some times when the buddhas come, known as the kalpas of the light, and when the buddhas don't appear in the world, known as the kalpas of the darkness.

There are lots of emperors of the world who have passed in earlier years, such as the emperors of the four golden continents, three silver continents, and the iron continent. In one of the earlier kalpas there was a great emperor who ruled the four continents, known as Nyima Chakra. This emperor, because of his previously created merits, had lots of queens and ministers and he had also 1,000 sons. During that emperor's kalpa of light, there came in that world Mahavairochana Buddha. To that great being the emperor served all the pleasures and worshipped him for many thousands of years.

The king, with great veneration, gave all his 1,000 sons to the great Mahavairochana Buddha and he told the great Mahavairochana, "I have heard that one thousand buddhas will appear. Maybe my sons will become the one thousand buddhas." At that time the great Mahavairochana said with a smile, "These one thousand sons will appear and slowly attain the highest enlightenment and benefit all sentient beings."

So the king put his sons' names in a golden urn and placed it before the great Buddha Shakyamuni Mahavairochana and the first buddha's name that came out was Krakucchanda, and the second name was Kanakamuni, and after that Mahakasyapa, the fourth Shakyamuni Buddha, and the fifth, the great Maitreya, the coming Buddha.

All the other Buddhas came during times when people enjoyed great endowments, but Shakyamuni came during a time when there was great degeneration. So he generated great compassion. When the degeneration of the five times slowly comes, there will be famine and wars and revolutions and all the workers of this world will diminish and the people will have great problems. At that time the emanation of Lord Maitreya Buddha comes and gives advice on morality and ethics, and slowly the environment improves and a time comes when people live up to 80,000 years …

The great Maitreya will appear in this world and achieve the great enlightenment. There are lots of Maitreya Buddha dharanis and mantras that we can recite …

The recitation of Maitreya's mantras gives a very good imprint in our mind for the future …

LAMA CHOBGYE RINPOCHE

Seeing Maitreya

In the sutras there are stories of devoted practitioners who meditate with the aspiration of actualizing Maitreya Buddha. One story tells of Asanga, a great pandit (learned philosopher) and a lineage lama of the graduated path to enlightenment.

Although Asanga meditated in a hermitage for twelve years in order to actualize the future Buddha, he did not see Maitreya. At the end of three years of retreat, Asanga became discouraged and left the hermitage. But he encountered something that inspired him to return there for another three years of retreat. He did this three more times, leaving and returning, but after twelve years still nothing had happened.

Finally Asanga abandoned his retreat and left the hermitage for the final time. As he was walking down the road, he saw a wounded dog, whose lower body had an open wound filled with maggots. On seeing the dog, Asanga experienced unbearable compassion. Deciding that the maggots would need food to live on, once he had picked them out of the wound, Asanga cut flesh from his own thigh and spread it out on the ground. He then picked up the maggots, but not with his fingers because he was afraid of crushing them. He closed his eyes and bent down to pick up the maggots with the tip of his tongue, but found that he could not reach them. There seemed to be nothing there. So he opened his eyes, and suddenly before him there was Maitreya Buddha.

Overwhelmed by the sudden appearance of Maitreya, Asanga asked the Buddha, "Why did you take so long to appear? I have been meditating on you for twelve years!"

Maitreya Buddha replied, " It is not that I was not here. I was here with you all the time, but you simply could not see me."

Asanga had the habit of spitting in the hermitage, and Maitreya proved that he had been in the room by showing Asanga the stains on his robes where he had spat on him.

Ngawang Rinzing Gytso Rinpoche is known as Charok Lama. Born on October 27, 1992, he is named after his previous incarnation.

Maitreya Buddha said, "I was always there, but you didn't see me because of your karmic obscurations. These obscurations have now been purified by your compassion. This is why you are now able to see me."

That one moment of intense compassion that Asanga felt toward the wounded dog completely purified his remaining negative karma, and he was able to see Maitreya Buddha – a realization denied him during twelve years of retreat.

Cherishing even one living being (whether a person or an animal) and sacrificing ourselves to take care of them brings about powerful purification – purifying all our negative karma, the cause of disease, and all our other problems. It heals our mind and our body. The story of Asanga stresses how essential it is for us to purify our negative obscurations, which prevent us from seeing the buddhas. Even when they are all around us, we cannot see them until we have completely purified ourselves. It is as if there is mist on the looking glass – everything is fogged up. Hence the emphasis on purification practices.

The tradition and everlasting benefits of holy objects

Buddhist tradition speaks of tremendous karmic merit to be gained by creating, and cherishing holy objects, and Buddhist history is replete with the remains of ancient Buddha images and statues, built since the time of Shakyamuni Buddha's enlightenment.

Countless images of Maitreya Buddha have been uncovered in various parts of Asia – for instance, in present-day Pakistan and in the National Museum of New Delhi are two fine examples of a standing Bodhisattva Maitreya dating from the second century BC. Historical texts also record the sighting of Maitreya images in India by the famous Chinese pilgrims Fa Hsien (fifth century AD) and Hsuan Tsang (seventh century). Both pilgrims report seeing a famous statue of Maitreya at the foot of a high mountain pass in northern Kashmir. According to legend, it was created by a sculptor who had observed the features of the future Buddha, after being magically transported to Maitreya's paradise realm of Tushita by the miraculous powers of a famous arhat. On his return from Tushita, the sculptor built an eight-foot (twenty-four-meter)-high statue in sandalwood, covered with gold plates.

This statue was built 300 years after the death of Shakyamuni Buddha, and it has been speculated that it was responsible for spreading the Mahayana teachings to Central Asia and China. Today, little trace remains of this once-famous statue. Indeed, few of the buddha images of Asia, built over the centuries and ravaged by the sands of time, still stand, although the ruins of Angkor Wat in Cambodia, and Borobodur on Indonesia's island of Java, bear testimony to the religious tradition of building buddha images.

This tradition is kept alive by Buddhist communities throughout the world. In Tibet a recent Panchen Lama built an 80-foot-high image of Maitreya cast in bronze at the Tashi Lhunpo monastery. In Nepal, two large Maitreya statues were built near the holy stupas of Swayambhunath and Bouddhanath, near Kathmandu. And in recent times two gigantic buddha statues were constructed, the most imposing being the inspiring Ushiku Buddha statue near Narita airport in Tokyo, Japan. Standing 394 feet (120 meters) high and completed in 1994, it is presently the largest statue of any kind in the world. The other statue, completed in the late 1980s, is the 80-foot-high seated image of Amitabha Buddha built on Lantau island, Hong Kong.

The two upmost decorative panels from the prayer hall at Kopan monastery display the Dharma wheel.

There is much karmic merit to be accumulated in building large buddha statues. According to the sutras, "The merits received in making a holy object are directly related to the number of atoms the holy object is composed of." And the larger the statue, the more people and animals who can see it. Building the giant Maitreya statue in Bodhgaya will enable many people to see it and thus accumulate merit.

It is also explained in the teachings that while holy objects exist, the teachings of Buddha will also exist and will continue to spread. It is said that the happiness of sentient beings depends on these teachings, and the existence of the teachings depends on having holy objects.

Making offerings to me now and making offerings

to a statue of me in the future will be of equal merit.

The result will be the same.

BUDDHA

Young thangka painters at work at the Traditional Thangka Painting School, Bhaktapur, Nepal.

Sentient beings who do not have the good fortune to actually see the Buddha need the holy objects of his body, speech, and mind, which become the field (object) for accumulating merit. Because of our obscurations and delusions, our minds, hearts, and bodies are still impure, and until we have purified ourselves we will never be able to see the buddhas in all their glorious form. So we "see" them in our minds, using our imagination and helped along by images of holy objects – statues, paintings, sculptures, and the ultimate holy object: gigantic buddha statues. When we make offerings to statues and images of Buddha, it is the same as if we are making offerings to Buddha himself.

And therein lie the precious benefits of books such as this – books filled with the beautiful images and precious teachings of the buddhas, which transform it into something special. When you view Dharma books in this way, you should treat them in the same way that you treat all holy objects: keeping them off the floor and surfaces where people sit, walk, and step; not placing other mundane things on top of them; not reading them in unsuitable places. And then reading books on the buddhas itself becomes a cause for enlightenment and rejoicing.

On Guru Devotion

I request you, kind Lord root guru
You, who are more extraordinary than all the buddhas,
Bless me that I am able to devote myself
To the qualified Lord guru in all my future lifetimes.

Whenever my guru gives me work, no matter how heavy the burden
Help me be like the earth, bearing all;
Whatever suffering, hardship, or problems occur
Help me be like the mountain, immovable.

That I shall be like a servant of a king
That I shall abandon pride and be like a sweeper
Holding the guru's work with joy and mind undisturbed.
That I shall be like a faithful dog, never responding with anger;
That I shall be like a boat to come and go for my guru.

O glorious and precious guru
Please bless me to be able to practice this way
May my devotion be forever like this.

Appendices

Making Mandala Offerings

Within Tibetan Buddhist practice, mandalas are symbolic representations of the universe purified. Generally, there are two primary contexts in which mandalas are used: one is the offering of the mandala (or universe) in a purified form to the gurus and buddhas as a way for the practitioner to develop generosity and overcome miserliness and avarice; the second, which is a part of Tantric practice, involves the visualization of the complete mandala (purified universe) of a buddha-deity, which includes the entire pure environment and its inhabitants.

The essence of the mandala is the realization of the spiritual force within the person performing the mandala meditation. I have seen Tibetan monks constructing a mandala of a specific buddha-deity, such as Kalachakra, with colored sand and the dust of precious stones. In recent years, His Holiness the Dalai Lama has introduced the stunningly beautiful Kalachakra mandala to the world during Kalachakra initiations he has given for Tibetan Buddhist practitioners in different parts of the globe. After the completion of the initiation ceremony or mandala exhibition, the mandala is ritually destroyed, expressing the impermanence of visible forms and symbolizing emptiness.

Mandala offering rings and gemstones are used to help visualize a purifed universe.

THE MANDALA OFFERING RITUAL

The mandala offering ritual described here is the most simple of mandala meditative visualization offerings. The symbolism of auspicious objects incorporated into the recitation part of the mandala ritual represents a simplifying of the three-dimensional mandala, which visually creates a perfect universe offered to Buddha or to our spiritual teachers.

In Tibetan Buddhism, the practice of offering the mandala is a ritual based on a mythological representation of the universe purified. It is based on the ancient cosmology in which our universe is seen as consisting of four major worlds, or continents, that surround the core of the universe in the form of the universal mountain, Mount Meru. All of these components rest on a golden base, or foundational ground, and are surrounded by an impenetrable vajra fence. Within this universe, then, are all the various perfect objects (of the five senses) and inhabitants that we offer to the buddhas and to our gurus. By offering, we relinquish our attachment, our sense of "ownership," to any of these things ... actually, to anything at all. For we have given it all away to the buddhas and to our gurus. In this way, we undermine and eventually eliminate altogether our deluded sense of "mine."

The mandala offering is so beautiful; it can be used by anyone. All it takes is a genuinely pure motivation to make the offering. And making mandala offerings is wonderfully physical – with a mandala set made up of a base (the golden ground) on which you build a wonderful pile of offerings, not only is your mind at work in imagining all these wonderful things, but your hands are put to work as well. You can make your own mandala set or you can purchase it from many Buddhist meditation centers.

THE MANDALA SET

This comprises:

The base
The three concentric rings
The Dharmachakra wheel
A cloth to cover or wrap the mandala set when not in use.

To create a mandala universe to offer, "fillers" are offered, which symbolize the contents of the mandala. What you use and how you combine them is up to you. I have seen stunningly beautiful mandala fillers made of special or colorful beads, and I have also seen very simple mandalas made of rice grains, which meant a great deal to their owners. The most important thing is the fillers should be visualized as precious offerings. Many people place pieces of jewellery inside their mandalas as well – rings, earrings, bracelets, and pendants. Others include special crystals and semi-precious stones.

After washing raw rice grains or uncooked seeds, with saffron water if possible, and allowing them to dry, the grains and seeds are ready for building the mandala.

The mandala sets available from most meditation centers come from either India or Nepal and they are often made of brass; some people choose to have the whole mandala set plated with real silver or gold. This is not necessary, however, as the gold can always be imagined.

Mandala sets should always be kept clean and treated with respect, wrapped in good-quality cloth, and kept inside a drawer.

CREATING THE MANDALA

1. *The person making the mandala offering takes a deep breath, clears their mind, and sits in a quiet corner, feeling comfortable and relaxed.*
2. *The cloth is placed flat on a low table or in the lap, with the mandala set laid out within easy reach. The fillers (rice grains, seeds, beads, or semi-precious stones) are placed on the cloth.*

3. Grain (or seeds, beads, and so on) are taken into the left palm and, using the same hand, the mandala base is held firmly, with the flat part of the base face upward.

4. Grain is taken with the right hand and put on the base, which is wiped three times in a circular clockwise direction with the forearm, tipping the grain away from the body. One thinks that they are correcting all improper motivation, and that the mandala that is about to be built will dissolve all negativities caused by one's own thoughts.

5. More grain is placed on the base. This time the base is wiped three times in a circular anti-clockwise direction with the forearm, tipping the grain toward the body. One thinks how the mandala offering is being made from their heart, and that they are receiving great and plentiful blessings from the buddhas of the ten directions.

6. Grain is spread over the base to symbolize the golden ground filled with all kinds of precious jewels. One thinks of this base as the mighty golden ground; Om Ah Hum is then recited three times. This is a simple blessing mantra, which ensures that no wandering spirits can disturb the practice or defile the mandala with bad energy. These three syllables should always be recited; this applies to all offerings placed on any altar.

7. The first ring is placed on the base and more grain is sprinkled around the inside of the ring. This symbolizes the parameters of one's mountain; the mighty iron fence around the edge of the Universe.

8. More grain, or a special symbol, is taken to represent the mountain in the center. This is Mount Meru, the king of mountains. It is the center of the world, the core of the universe.

9. More grain is sprinkled into the ring to represent the continent of the East. (Note that East is toward the body if the motivation is to receive auspicious blessing chi; and away from the body if the aim is to overcome one's negativities.)

10. More grain is put into the ring to signify the continent of the South.

11. More grain is put into the ring to signify the continent of the West.

12. More grain is put into the ring to signify the continent of the North.

13. More grain is put into the ring to signify the subcontinents of the East.

14. More grain is put into the ring to signify the subcontinents of the South.

15. More grain is put into the ring to signify the subcontinents of the West.

16. More grain is put into the ring to signify the subcontinents of the North.

17. More grain is put into the ring to signify the precious mountain.

18. More grain is put into the ring to signify the wish-granting tree.

19. More grain is put into the ring to signify the wish-fulfilling cow.

20. More grain is put into the ring to signify the unploughed harvest.

21. *The second ring is placed on top of the grain-filled first ring. One thinks how they are placing eight precious objects belonging to a wheel-turning king who rules the four continents.*

22. *More grain is put into the ring to signify the precious wheel.*

23. *More grain is put into the ring to signify the precious jewel.*

24. *More grain is put into the ring to signify the precious queen.*

25. *More grain is put into the ring to signify the precious minister.*

26. *More grain is put into the ring to signify the precious elephant.*

27. *More grain is put into the ring to signify the precious horse.*

28. *More grain is put into the ring to signify the precious general.*

29. *More grain is put into the ring to signify the great treasure vase.*

30. *More grain is taken and placed in the inner area of the second ring. One imagines eight beautiful offering goddesses carry eight different types of offering; the goddesses are visualized as the grains are placed into the ring. The first is the goddess of beauty; the second is the goddess of garlands; the third is the goddess of songs; the fourth is the goddess of dance; the fifth is the goddess of flowers; the sixth is the goddess of incense; the seventh is the goddess of light; the eighth is the goddess of perfume.*

31. *The third ring is placed on the grain-filled second ring.*

32. *More grain is placed into the ring. To the left of the person doing the offering, it signifies the sun; to their right, the moon.*

33. *More grain is put into the ring to signify the precious parasol. This is a symbol of protection, protecting against obstacles and bad luck; the whole universe is protected by this divine umbrella.*

34. *More grain is put into the ring to signify the banner of victory. One thinks how they are receiving plenty of auspicious blessings from the buddhas.*

35. *The Dharmachakra (wheel) is placed in the middle, at the top of the grain-filled third ring, to represent the peak of the mandala. In the center here are the most perfect riches of gods and humans. There is nothing missing; everything is pure and delightful.*

As the mandala offering is constructed, one visualizes all the other people in the universe, each one of you offering many, many mandalas that fill all of space.

Requests or dedications are made, then the grains of the mandala are tipping toward the body, as one thinks at the same time how they are receiving all the blessings of the buddhas and their guru. Brilliant white light is visualized, emanating from the mandala and entering through the crown chakra, at the top of the head, completely filling the body and mind and purifying all the obstacles formed by negativities within. When the grains are tipped toward the body, the mandala collapses, signifying the impermanence of everything.

Glossary

Skt = Sanskrit; Tib. = Tibetan

aggregates	The associated components of body and mind; a person comprises five aggregates: form, feeling, discrimination, thoughts, and consciousness.
arhat	(Skt) Literally, "foe-destroyer." A monk who has destroyed his delusions and attained liberation from samsara, becoming a saint. (This is not, however, the attainment of complete enlightenment.)
Avalokiteshvara	*See* Chenrezig.
bodhichitta	(Skt) The altruistic aspiration to achieve enlightenment in order to liberate all living beings from suffering – a vital component in the attainment of enlightenment.
bodhisattva	(Skt) A compassionate being who possesses bodhichitta.
Boudhanath	A village just outside Kathmandu built around the Boudhanath stupa, a famous Buddhist pilgrimage site.
Brahma	A powerful Hindu deity in the god realm.
buddha	(Skt) A fully enlightened being; the term also refers to Shakyamuni, the historical Buddha. *See* Enlightenment; Guru Shakyamuni Buddha.
buddha-nature	The emptiness, or ultimate nature, of the mind combined with bodhichitta. Every sentient being possesses the potential to become fully enlightened – a buddha.
chakra	One of the body's energy centers. There are seven chakras in the human body.
Chenrezig	(Tib.) Also Avalokiteshvara (Skt). The Buddha of Compassion; the male meditation deity who embodies fully enlightened compassion. The Dalai Lamas are said to be emanations of this buddha. The Chinese equivalent is the Goddess of Mercy, Kuan Yin.
clear light	The most subtle state of mind, achieved when all the energy-winds have dissolved into the central channel, as happens during death; this is utilized in meditation by accomplished Tantric practitioners.
cyclic existence	*See* Samsara.
dakini	A fairy maiden from the Pure Land who has come down to the human realm.
delusions	The negative states of mind that are the cause of suffering. The five delusions are anger, ignorance, pride and miserliness, jealousy, and attachment.
dependent-arising	Knowing that the existence of self is dependent on, and related to others and other objects.
devadatta	Shakyamuni's cousin, who was jealous of the Buddha and constantly tried to harm him.
Dharma	(Skt) literally, "phenomenon". In general, the spiritual practice; specifically, the practice of Buddha's teachings, Buddhadharma.
Dharmakaya	(Skt) The omniscient (holy) mind of a buddha.
disturbing thoughts	*See* Delusions.
disturbing-thought obscurations	The delusions that obstruct or create obstacles to the attainment of liberation.
eight freedoms	The eight states that a perfect human rebirth is free from – that is: (1) freedom from being born in a hell realm; (2) freedom from being born as a hungry ghost; (3) freedom from being born as an animal; (4) freedom from being born as a long-life god; (5) freedom from being born as a barbarian; (6) freedom from holding wrong views; (7) freedom from being born in a dark age when no Buddha has descended; (8) freedom from being born with defective mental or physical faculties.
emptiness	The absence, or lack of, true existence. Ultimately, every phenomenon is empty of existing truly, or from its own side, or independently.
enlightenment	Buddhahood; omniscience; full awakening. The ultimate goal of Mahayana Buddhist practice, attained when all limitations have been removed from the mind and all positive potential has been realized. A state characterized by unlimited compassion, skill, and wisdom.
five delusions	*See* Delusions.
five extreme negativities (uninterrupted negative karma)	Killing one's father, one's mother, or an arhat; maliciously drawing blood from a buddha; causing division within the Sangha.
five precepts	The vows taken by lay Buddhist practitioners: no killing, no stealing, no lying, no sexual misconduct, no intoxicants.
four elements	Earth, water, fire, and air, or wind.
Four Noble Truths	The subject of the Buddha's first discourse: true suffering, the true cause of suffering, the true cessation of suffering, and the true path to the cessation of suffering.
from happiness to happiness	From one happiness to the next, from liberation from samsara to the attainment of enlightenment.

Gelug	(Tib.) The Virtuous Order; the order of Tibetan Buddhism founded by Lama Tsongkhapa and his disciples in the early fifteenth century.
gompa	The prayer hall of a Buddhist monastery or meditation center.
graduated path to enlightenment	Or Lam-Rim (Tib.). Originally outlined in Tibet by Lama Atisha in the Lamp of the Path to Enlightenment, the graduated path is a step-by-step presentation of the Buddha's teachings.
guru	A spiritual teacher, known in Tibet as a lama.
Guru Shakyamuni Buddha	(563–483 bc) The fourth of the 1,000 founding buddhas of this present world age. He was born a prince of the Shakya clan in northern India, and taught the sutras and the Tantric path to liberation and full enlightenment.
guru yoga	A special devotional practice in praise and respect to the gurus to develop guru devotion, which is the foundation of the path to enlightenment.
Heart Sutra	Also known as The Essence of Wisdom. Recited daily by many Buddhist practitioners, this is the shortest of the Perfection of Wisdom texts.
hell being	A samsaric being in the realm of greatest suffering.
Hinayana	(Skt) Literally, the "Lesser Vehicle." The path of the arhats, the ultimate goal being nirvana.
imprint	The seed, or potential, left on the mind by positive or negative actions of body, speech, and mind.
Jatakatales	Moralistic birth stories relating to the Buddha.
Kadampa	See Lama Atisha.
Kalachakra	(Skt) Literally, "wheel of time." A male meditation deity of the Highest Yoga Tantra. Kalachakra initiations from His Holiness the Dalai Lama have brought this practice to many thousands of people.
karma	(Skt) Literally, "action." The law of cause and effect: the process whereby virtuous actions of body, speech, and mind lead to happiness, and non-virtuous ones to suffering.
kata	A traditional silk scarf given in Tibetan ritual.
Kopan monastery	The monastery founded in 1970 by Lama Thubten Yeshe and Lama Kyabje Zopa Rinpoche near Bouddhanath in the Kathmandu valley, Nepal.
lama	(Tib.) Literally, "heavy," as in heavy with Dharma knowledge. The Tibetan word for a guru.
Lama Atisha	(982–1054) The renowned Indian Buddhist master who came to Tibet to help in the revival of Buddhism and established the Kadampa tradition. His Lamp of the Path to Enlightenment was the first Lam-Rim text.
Lama Tsongkhapa	(1357–1419) The revered teacher and accomplished practitioner who founded the Gelug order of Tibetan Buddhism. An emanation of Manjushri, the Buddha of Wisdom.
Lam-Rim	(Tib.) See Graduated path to enlightenment.
Lawado cave	The cave in the Solu Khumbu region of Nepal where the Lawudo lama lived and meditated for many years. Lama Kyabje Zopa Rinpoche is recognized as the reincarnation of the Lawudo lama.
liberation	The state of complete freedom from samsaric existence; nirvana, the state beyond sorrow; the goal of the Hinayana practitioner.
lineage lamas	The spiritual teachers who constitute the line of direct guru–disciple transmission, from Shakyamuni Buddha to the teachers of the present day.
lower realms	The three realms of cyclic existence with the most suffering: the hell realm, the realm of the hungry ghosts, and the animal realm; see Samsara.
Mahayana	(Skt) Literally, the "Great Vehicle" school of Buddhism. The path of the bodhisattvas, the ultimate goal being buddhahood.
Maitreya Buddha	(Skt) Literally, the "Loving One." The next buddha after Shakyamuni, and the fifth of the 1,000 buddhas of this world age.
mala	(Skt) A rosary used for counting mantras; one mala comprises 108 repeats.
mandala	A circle or meditative pattern conveying ancient knowledge of the creation of the Universe; the search for self; also a spiritually visualized palace or entourage of a buddha.
mantra	(Skt) Literally, "protection of the mind." Sanskrit syllables recited in conjunction with the practice of a particular meditation deity and embodying the qualities of that deity.
Mara	A disturbing force of delusion; an enemy of the mind.
merit	The positive energy accumulated in the mind as a result of virtuous actions of body, speech, and mind.
migratory beings	Another term for sentient beings, who migrate from rebirth to rebirth within the Six Realms of Existence.
Milarepa	(1040–1123) A great ascetic Tibetan yogi and poet, the foremost disciple of Marpa. He was famous for his intense practice, his devotion to his guru, his many songs of spiritual realization, and his attainment of enlightenment in one lifetime.
mudra	A ritual hand gesture or movement.
Nagarjuna	The great Indian scholar and Tantric adept who lived approximately 400 years after Buddha's death. Propounder of the Middle Way, he clarified the ultimate meaning of Buddha's teachings on emptiness.
nirvana	(Skt) See Liberation.
obscurations	The subtle defilements of the mind that obstruct the attainment of enlightenment.

om mani padme hum	The mantra of Chenrezig, the Buddha of Compassion.
omniscient mind	*See* Enlightenment.
Padmasambhava	The eighth-century Indian Tantric master who was mainly responsible for the establishment of Buddhism in Tibet. He is revered by all Tibetan Buddhists, especially the practitioners of the Nyingma school.
pandit	(Skt) A highly learned philosopher.
Paramitas	(Skt) Perfections; the practices of a bodhisattva. On the basis of bodhichitta, a bodhisattva practices the Six Perfections: generosity, morality, patience, enthusiastic perseverance, concentration, and wisdom.
parinirvana	Complete nirvana or liberation.
perfect human rebirth	*See* Precious human body.
Perfection of Wisdom	Or Prajnaparamita (Skt). The teachings of Shakyamuni Buddha, in which the wisdom of emptiness and the path of the bodhisattva are explained.
Perfections	*See* Paramitas.
Prajnaparamita	(Skt) See Perfection of Wisdom. Also the name of the female deity who embodies wisdom.
precepts	*See* Five precepts.
precious human body	The rare human state, qualified by the eight freedoms and ten richnesses, that is the ideal condition for practicing Dharma and achieving enlightenment.
preliminary practices	The meditations for removing hindrances and accumulating merit, so that a disciple will have success in the practice of Tantra.
preta	(Skt) A hungry ghost. One of the six classes of samsaric beings, pretas experience the greatest sufferings of hunger and thirst.
puja	(Skt) A religious ceremony; an offering prayer ritual.
Pure Land	From the Tibetan word Sukhavati, meaning "happy" or "pure land" – the western paradise of the Buddha Amitabha. Pure Land Buddhism is devotional Buddhism offering escape from samsara through faith in a deified Buddha, and is widely practiced in China, Korea, and Japan.
purification	The removal, or cleansing, of negative karma and its imprints from the mind.
refuge	The heartfelt reliance upon the Buddha, Dharma, and Sangha for guidance on the path to enlightenment. Taking refuge with a guru is the process of officially becoming his student, thereby entering into a guru–disciple relationship.
renunciation	The state of mind of wishing to be liberated from samsara because of not having, for even one second, the slightest attraction to samsaric perfections.
Rinpoche	(Tib.) Literally, "precious one." An honorific term usually given to recognized reincarnate lamas; also a respectful title for one's own lama.
rupa	A statue.
Rupakaya	(Skt) The pure (holy) body of an enlightened being, of which there are two aspects: sambhogakaya and nirmanakaya.
sadhana	A meditative visualization; a spiritual practice leading to perfection.
samsara	(Skt) Cyclic existence; the recurring cycle of birth, death, and rebirth within one or other of the Six Realms of Existence, under the control of karma and delusions; also refers to the contaminated aggregates of a sentient being.
Sangha	(Skt) In general, refers to the ordained community of monks and nuns; absolute Sangha refers to those who have directly realized emptiness.
seed-syllable	The special Tibetan or Sanskrit syllable of each buddha deity.
sentient being	Any being within the Six Realms of Existence who has not yet reached enlightenment.
Sera monastery	One of the three great Gelug monasteries, originally situated north of Lhasa in Tibet. It was founded by Jamchen Choje, a disciple of Lama Tsong Khapa; now re-established in southern India.
Shakyamuni Buddha	*See* Guru Shakyamuni Buddha.
Six Realms of Existence	Comprises the upper realms of gods, demi-gods, and humans, plus the lower realms of animals, hungry ghosts, and hell beings.
Six Perfections	*See* Paramitas.
stupa	(Skt) A reliquary representing the Buddha's mind.
suffering migratory being	A being born in the animal, hungry ghost, or hell realms.
Sukhavati	*See* Pure Land.
Sunyata	(Skt) Meaning the emptiness of all things.
sutras	(Skt) The Hinayana and Paramitayana discourses of the Buddha; a scriptural text and the teachings and practices that it contains – for example, the Diamond Cutter and Perfection of Wisdom sutras.
sutta	A discourse of the Pali canon.
Tantra	(Skt) The esoteric discourses of the Buddha; a scriptural text and the teachings and practices that it contains. Tantric practices generally involve identification of oneself with a fully enlightened deity in order to transform one's impure states of body, speech, and mind into the pure state of an enlightened being. Also a school of the Mahayana tradition that greatly influenced Tibetan Buddhism.

Tara	(Skt) A female meditation deity who embodies the enlightened activity of the buddhas; often referred to as the mother of the buddhas of the past, present, and future.
tathagata	An exalted One; a buddha.
ten richnesses	The ten qualities that characterize a perfect human rebirth: (1) being born as a human being; (2) being born in a Dharma country; (3) being born with perfect mental and physical faculties; (4) being free of the five extreme negativities; (5) having faith in the Buddha's teachings; (6) being born when a buddha has descended; (7) being born when the teachings have been revealed; (8) being born when the teachings are still alive; (9) being born when there are still followers of the teachings; (10) having the necessary conditions to practice Dharma.
thangka	A devotional painting of buddha images on cloth.
thought transformation	Or lo-jong (Tib.). A powerful approach to the development of bodhichitta, in which the mind is trained to use all situations (both happy and unhappy) as a means to destroy self-cherishing.
three poisons	Desire, anger, and ignorance.
tsa-tsa	A miniature buddha image.
tulku	A reincarnate lama.
unification of no more learning	The ultimate achievement, buddhahood.
uninterrupted negative karma	*See* Five extreme negativities.
universal king	Also wheel-turning king; a powerful king who propagates the Dharma.
upper realms	The three realms of cyclic existence where there is greater happiness and less suffering: the god, the demi-god, and human realms.
Vajrasattva	(Skt) A Tantric deity used in purification practices.
Vajrayana	(Skt) The quickest vehicle of Buddhism, capable of leading to the attainment of full enlightenment within one lifetime. Also known as Tantrayana and Mantrayana.
yogi	(Skt) A highly realized meditator; a spiritual practitioner.

ACKNOWLEDGMENTS

I thank from my heart the Venerable Roger Kunsang, who inspired this book. Thank you for what you do and who you are. I thank the Venerable Marcel Bertels and the Venerable Holly Ansett for their guidance and friendship; the Venerable Connie Miller, Venerable Sarah Thresher and Merry Colony for checking through the text; and my very dear Dharma friends whose presence in my life has enriched it considerably with the things that matter. Many grateful thanks to Lama Lhundrup Khen Rinpoche, the abbot of Kopan Monastery for kindly allowing access to take these magnificent pictures; to Venerable Nyima Tashi for being an invaluable guide and to little Charok Lama for just being there.

I thank also Belinda Budge, my Publishing Director, for helping me conceive this book; my friend and editor, Liz Dean, who polishes my words and images; and the great team at Element, HarperCollins led by Clare Pemberton. Those who want more mantras and practices can write directly to the Foundation for the Preservation of the Mahayan Tradition (FPMT) at: FPMT, Inc., Education Department, 125B La Posta Road PO Box 888, Taos, NM 87571, USA. Tel: 1 505 758 7766, ext. 124. Fax: 1 505 758 7765. Email: materials@fpmt.org.

All author royalties from this book will be donated to Dharma Charitable activities under the guidance of Lama Kyabje Zopa Rinpoche.

The publishers would like to thank the following for their valuable assistance with photography: Kay Curtis; the Traditional Thanka Painting School, Tripura Sundari (Tulachhen)-10, Bhaktapur, Nepal; Kirti Shakya and Gautam Shakya of Statues House, 5/30 Taphalon, Jawalakhel, Patan, Nepal; Surendra and Pradip of Tibetan Thanka Treasure, PO Box 5336, Thamel Kathmandu, Nepal; Manoh Tamrakar and all at Nepalese Crafts (P) Ltd, Patan Industrial Estate Lagankhel, Patan, Nepal, and the staff of the Yak and Yeti Hotel, Kathmandu.

Photography Credits

Page 29, Lama Kyabje Zopa Rinpoche © Pat Goh

Pages xii, 37, 97, 98–99, 128, 162, 169, 231 © The Venerable Roger Kunsang.

All other photography by Geoff Dann.

Author website: www.Lillian-Too.com

Feng Shui website: www.wofs.com

Buddhist website: www.lamazopa.com

Worldwide FPMT Offices

American Regional Office
1195 Fynes Ct.,
San Jose, CA 95131, USA
Tel: (1) (408) 437 9373
Email: bonniebaptist@hotmail.com
Coordinator: Bonnie Baptist

Asia Pacific Regional Office
#16-05, Mirage Tower,
80 Kim Seng Road,
Singapore 239 426
Tel: (65) 6235 0647
Email: bopbop@singnet.com.sg
Coordinator: Doris Low

European Regional Office
"Reynies," Route de Castres
81500 Lavaur, France
Tel: (33) (5) 63 58 66 311
Email: martinfishter@compuserve.com
Coordinator: Martin Fishter

Australian National Office
P.O. Box 2020

Windsor, QLD 4030, Australia
Tel: (61) (7) 3632 8321
Fax: (61) (7) 3857 8040
Email: fpmtnatoffice@iprimus.com.au
Coordinator: Sally Dudgeon

International Mahayana Institute
c/o Nalanda Monastery
Chateau Rouzegas
81500 Lavaur, France
Tel: (33) (5) 63 58 02 25
Fax: (33) (5) 63 58 19 87
Email: chantalcar@wanadoo.fr
Director: Ven. Chantal Carrerot
Secretary: Ven. Lhundub Chonyi

International Office
P.O. Box 888
Taos, NM 87571, USA
Tel: (1) (505) 758 7766
Fax: (1) (505) 758 7765
Email: fpmtinfo@fpmt.org
www.fpmt.org
Executive Director: Massimo Corona

Italian National Office
Via Cortine 8
Barberino Val d'Elsa
Florence, 50021
Italy
Tel: (39) (55) 807 5732
Fax: (39) (57) 793 3831
Email:macini@libero.it
Coordinator: Giovanna Pescetti

New Zealand National Office
PO Box 3319
Richmond, Nelson
New Zealand
Tel (64) (3) 543 2015
Fax (64) (3) 543 2016
Email: chandrakirti@tasman.net
Coordinator: Bruce Farley

South Asian Regional Office
c/o Himalayan Buddhist Meditation
Centre
Kamaladi Ganesthan
PO Box 817, Kathmandu, Nepal

Tel: (977) (1) 221 875
Fax: (977) (1) 251 409
Email: hbmc@mos.com.np
Coordinator: Pooja Manandhar

Spanish National Office
c/o Nagarjuna C.E.T. Madrid
C/Duque de Osuna, 8, Ext., 2º Izq.
28015 Madrid, Spain
Tel/Fax: (34)(91) 541 37 55
Email: nagarma@batch-pc.es
Coordinator: Marion Lambert

Taiwan National Office
1F, No. 3, Alley 14,
Lane 75, Sec. 4, Nan-Jing East Road,
Taipei 105
Taiwan, R.O.C.
Tel: (886) (2) 8770 6939
Fax: (886) (2) 2546 9923
Email: fpmttw@ms22.hinet.net
Coordinator: Klaus Liu

Worldwide FPMT Centers and Study Groups

AUSTRALIA 61
Atisha Centre
RMB 1530, Eaglehawk, VIC 3556
Tel/Fax: (03) 5446 3336
Email: atisha_office@impulse.net.au
www.atisha.tripod.com
Director: Ian Green

Buddha House
3 Nelson Street
Fullarton, SA 5063
Tel: (08) 8379 9153
Fax: (08) 8379 9511
Email: buddhahouse@senet.com.au
www.buddhahouse.asn.au
Director: Gabe Edwards
Resident teacher: Geshe Pema Tsering

Chag-tong Chen-tong Centre
PO Box 195
Snug, TAS 7054
Tel: (03) 6267 9203

Email: chagtong@aol.com
Director: Lindy Mailhot

Chengawa Centre
PO Box 3017
Manuka, ACT 2603
Tel: (02) 6295 0157
Email: sjhunter@cybermac.com.au
Director: Sue Hunter

Chenrezig Institute
PO Box 41
Eudlo, QLD 4554
Tel: (07) 5445 0077
Fax: (07) 5445 0088
Email: info@chenrezig.com.au
www.chenrezig.com.au
Director: Colin Crosbie
Resident teacher: Geshe Tashi Tsering

Chenrezig Nuns Community
PO Box 41, Eudlo, QLD 4554
Tel: (07) 5445 0077
Fax: (07) 5445 0088
Email: info@chenrezig.com.au
Manager: Ven. Yeshe Khadro

Two projects of Chenrezig Institute:
The Enlightenment Project for Purification
and Merit
PO Box 41, Eudlo, QLD 4554
Tel: (07) 5445 0077
Fax: (07) 5445 0088
Email: enlightenmentproject
@compuserve.com
www.fpmt.org/enlightenment
Manager: Gayle Laverty

The Garden of Enlightenment
PO Box 41
Eudlo, QLD 4554
Tel: (07) 5445 0077

Fax: (07) 5445 0088
Email: foulkes@worldoptions.com.au
www.chenrezig.com.au/indexge.htm
Manager: Garrey Foulkes

Cittamani Hospice Service
PO Box 324
Palmwoods, QLD 4555
Tel: (07) 5445 0822
Fax: (07) 5445 0688
Email:
cittamanihospice@powerup.com.au
Director: Alex Moore

De-Tong Ling Retreat Centre
R.S.D. 418
via Kingscote, SA 5223
Tel: (08) 8559 3276
Email: kcuddihy@kin.net.au
www.detongling.org
Director: Kimball Cuddihy

Dromtonpa Study Group
PO Box 66,
Hepburn Springs,
VIC 3461
Tel/Fax: (03) 5348 7554
Email: dmzeh@netconnect.com.au
Coordinator: Marita Zeh

Hayagriva Buddhist Centre
64 Banksia Tce
Kensington, (put comma in) WA 6151
Tel/Fax: (08) 9367 4817
Email: leuba@iinet.net.au
www.welcome.to/fpmt-hayagriva
Director: Luba McMaugh

Hospice of Mother Tara
Unit 3/2B Victoria Street
Bunbury, WA 6230
Tel: (08) 9791 9798
Fax: (08) 9721 9497
Email: Glenda.lee@bigpond.com
www.Aphrodite.curtin.edu.au/callum/bu
dd.html
Director: Glenda Lee

Kadam Sharawa Study Group
17 Plateau Road
North Gosford, NSW 2250
Tel: (02) 4324 8860
Email: kadamsharawa@yahoo.com
www.geocities.com/kadamsharawa
Coordinator: Jill Grosche

Karuna Hospice Service
PO Box 2020
Windsor, QLD 4030
Tel: (07) 3632 8300
Fax: (07) 3857 8040
Email: karuna@karuna.org.au
Director: Ven. Yeshe Khadro

Langri Tangpa Centre
51 Enoggera Road
Newmarket, QLD 4051
Tel/Fax: (07) 3356 9523
Email: langritangpa@iprimus.com.au
www.buddhanet.net/langri-tangpa.htm
Director: Michael Bouwman

Rigsum Gonpo
25 Kiernan Street
Manuda, QLD 4870
Tel: (07) 4053 2915
Email: rigsumgonpo@hotmail.com
Director: Geri LeVinge

Shen Phen Ling Study Group
PO Box 178, Wondonga, VIC 3689
Tel: (02) 6033 2355
Email: emowlam@iprimus.com.au
Coordinator: Libby Mowlam

Tara Institute
3 Mavis Ave, Brighton East, VIC 3187
Tel: (03) 9596 8900
Fax: (03) 9596 4856
Email: admin@tarainstitute.com.au
www.tarainstitute.com.au
Director: David Andrews
Resident teacher: Geshe Lobsang Doga

Thubten Shedrup Ling
RMB 1530, Eaglehawk, VIC 3556
Tel/Fax: (03) 5446 3691
Email: tsl@impulse.net.au
www.atisha.tripod.com/monastery.html
Director: Ven. Dennis Kenny

Tse Chen Cho Khor Stupa
16 Brodie Street, Bendigo VIC 3550
Tel: (04) 1739 8877
Email: iang@cgm.com.au
www.stupa.org.au
Director: Ian Green

Vajrasattva Mountain Centre
155 Lurline St.
Katoomba, NSW 2780
Tel/Fax: (02) 4782 1931
Email: vajrasat@bigpond.com.au
www.users.bigpond.com/vajrasat/
Director: Ven. Norma Brahatis

Vajrayana Institute
PO Box 408, Newtown, NSW 2042
Tel: (02) 9550 2066
Fax: (02) 9550 4966
Email: office@vajrayana.com.au
Director: Cheryl Gough

AUSTRIA (43)
Panchen Losang Chogyen Study Group
Naaffgasse 18
Vienna A-1180
Tel: (1) 479 24 22
Email: a.husnik@utanet.at
Coordinator: Andrea Husnik

BRAZIL 55
Centro Shiwa Lha
Rua Almirante Tamandaré
66-sala 505, 20031-970, Flamengo
Rio de Janeiro, cep 22210-060

Tel: (21) 261 9399
Fax: (21) 224 2142
Email: Shiwalha@marlin.com.br
Director: Nilcea Mesquite

Kalachakra Study Group
Rua Abdon Batista 121
Sala 1509, Apt. 1003, Centro-Joinville
Santa Catarina State
cep 89201-010
Tel: (47) 455 0506
Email: sgouveas@uol.com.br
Coordinator: Sergio Gouveas

Naljorma Study Group
Av. Manoel Dias da Silva, 2157
Ed. Esplanada Ave., sala 512,
Pituba Salvador
Bahia 41830-001
Tel: (071) 240-7252
Email: Tshanti1@aol.com
Coordinators: Tania Belfort and Zenaide
Moret

CANADA 1
Kachoe Zung Juk Ling Abbey
2077 153rd Street
Surrey, B.C., V4A 8M8
Tel/Fax: (604) 541 8797
Email: AnilaAnnMcNeil@telus.net
http://kzjling.abbey.canada.tripod.com/
Director: Ven. Ann McNeil

Lama Yeshe Ling Study Group
28 Eby St. N. Kitchener
Ontario N2H 2V7
Tel: (519) 741-8673
Email: info@lamayesheling.org
http://www.lamayesheling.org/
Coordinator: Lynn Shwadchuck

CHINA 852
Cham-Tse-Ling
3/F., Block A, 3 Lau Sin St.,
Park View Mansion,
North Point, Hong Kong
Tel: 2770 7239
Fax: 2488 9299
Email: info@fpmtmba.org.hk
www.fpmtmba.org.hk
Co-directors: Ven. Tenzin Pemba and
Esther Ngai

COLOMBIA 57
Centro Yamantaka
Calle 122, No. 40-22
Bogotá

Tel: 1 213 70 66
Email: fpmt@telesat.com.co
www.geocities.com/Athens/Oracle/4570
Director: Mauricio Roa MacKenzie

DENMARK 45
Tong-nyi Nying-je Ling
Klerkegade 12, st.
1308 Copenhagen K
Tel/Fax: 32 54 31 58
Email lise-lotte.design@get2net.dk
Director: Lise-Lotte Kolb

A project of Tong-nyi Nying-je Ling
The Center for Conscious Living and Dying
Klerkegade 12, st.
1308 Copenhagen K
Tel/Fax: 33 13 11 08
Email: cld@mobilixnet.dk
Coordinator: Maria Damsholt

EL SALVADOR (503)
Kusum Ling Study Group
Pasaje Guatavita # 4
San Salvador
Tel: 273-3723
Email: gsoriano@sv.cciglobal.net
Coordinator: Gustavo Soriano

ENGLAND 44
Jamyang Buddhist Centre
The Old Courthouse
43 Renfrew Road, London SE11 4NA
Tel: (0207) 820 8787
Fax: (0207) 820 8605
Email: admin@jamyang.co.uk
www.jamyang.co.uk
Director: Alison Murdoch
Resident teacher: Geshe Tashi Tsering

Jamyang Buddhist Centre Leeds
95 Harehills Avenue,
Leeds LS8 4ET
Tel: (0113) 262 0564
Email: admin@jamyangleeds.fsnet.co.uk
www.jamyangleeds.org
Director: Jan Metcalfe

Shen Phen Thubten Choeling Centre for
socially and ecologically-engaged
Buddhism
Nurses Cottage
Long Lane, Peterchurch
Hereford HR2 0TE
Tel/Fax: (01981) 550 246
Email: greengate@gn.apc.org
Director: Paul Swatridge

FRANCE 33

Editions Vajra Yogini
Chateau d'en Clausade
Marzens, 81500 Lavaur
Tel: (05) 63 58 17 22
Fax: (05) 63 58 03 48
Email: contacts@vajra-yogini.com
www.vajra-yogini.com
Coordinator: Michel Henry

Institut Vajra Yogini
Chateau d'en Clausade
Marzens, 81500 Lavaur
Tel: (05) 63 58 17 22
Fax: (05) 63 58 03 48
Email: institut.vajra.yogini@wanadoo.fr
Director: Francois Lecointre
Resident teacher: Geshe Losang Tengye

Kalachakra Centre
5 passage Delessert,75010 Paris
Tel/Fax: (01) 40 05 02 22
Email: kalachakra@multimania.com
www.multimania.com/kalachakra
Director: Ven. Elisabeth Drukier

Nalanda Monastery
Château Rouzegas
Labastide St. Georges
81500 Lavaur
Tel: (05) 63 58 02 25
Fax: (05) 63 58 19 87
Email: nalanda@compuserve.com
www.nalanda-monastery.org
Director: Ven. Jean-François Bergevin
Resident teacher: Geshe Losang Jamphel

FRENCH POLYNESIA 689

Naropa Meditation Center
Papara, PK 35, 5 Côté mer
PO Box 20610
98713 Papeete - Tahiti
Tel: 54 72 88
Email: rcf.tahiti@mail.pf
Director: Brenda Chin-Foo

GERMANY 49

Aryatara Institut
Barerstraße 70/Rgb.
80799 München
Tel: (089) 2781 7227
Fax: (089) 2781 7226
Email: aryatara@aol.com
www.aryatara.de
Director: Alnis Grants
Resident teacher: Geshe Soepa

GUATEMALA 502

Losang Chogyel Grupo de Estudio
5 calle 2-80 zona 1
Guatemala City, Guatemala
Tel: 515-29-57
Email: losangchogyel@terra.com
Coordinator: Igor Sarmientos

INDIA 91

Lotsawa Rinchen Zangpo Translator
Programme
Tipa Road, House No. 1110
McLeod Ganj, Dharamsala
Kangra District, HP 176 219
Tel: (1892) 21094
Fax: (1892) 21681
Email: lrztp@vsnl.com
Director: Elea Redel

Maitreya Project Universal
Education School
P O Bodhgaya, Gaya District
Bihar, 824 231
Tel: (631) 200 330/200 058
Fax: (631) 200 774
Email: School@maitreyaproject.org
Director: Dick Jeffrey

Maitri Charitable Trust
PO Box 32
Bodhgaya, Gaya District, Bihar 824 231
Tel: (631) 200 841
Fax: (631) 201 946
Email: ferranti@vsnl.net
www.fpmt.org/maitri
Director: Adriana Ferranti

Osel Study Group
Buddha House, Muddi Zor
Anjuna
Goa 403 509
Tel: 832 27 3934
Email: oselingoa@yahoo.co.in
Coordinator: Sonam Bist

Root Institute
Bodhgaya, Gaya District
Bihar 824 231
Tel: (631) 200 714
Fax: (631) 200 548
Email: rootinstitute@vsnl.net
www.rootinstitute.com
Director: Trisha Donnelly

Sera IMI House
Shedrup Sungdrel Ling

88 Sera Je Monastery
PO Bylakuppe 571104
Karnataka
Email: SeraIMIhouse@yahoo.com
www.SeraIMIhouse.org
Director: Ven. Fedor Stracke

Shakyamuni Buddha Community
Health Care Centre
Bodhgaya, Gaya District
Bihar 824 231
Tel: (631) 200 714
Fax: (631) 200 548
Director: Trisha Donnelly

Tushita Mahayana Meditation Centre
9 Padmini Enclave, Hauz Khas
New Delhi 110 016
Tel: (11) 651 3400
Fax: (11) 469 2963
Email: renukas@del2.vsnl.net.in
http://www.tmmc.tripod.com
Director: Renuka Singh

Tushita Meditation Centre
McLeod Ganj, Dharamsala
Kangra District, HP 176 219
Tel: (1892) 21866
Fax: (1892) 21246 Attn Tushita
Email: tushita1@vsnl.com
www.tushita.info
Director: Ven. Anet Engel

INDONESIA 62

Potowa Center
Jl. Kepa Duri Mas
Block JJ No.1
Jakarta Barat 11510
Tel: (0) (0818) 955 998
Email: potowa@cbn.net.id
Director: Teddy Leo

ITALY 39

"0" to be dialed when calling Italy
(after "39")
Centro Lama Tzong Khapa
Via General Pennella 12
21100 Treviso
Tel: (0422) 303 436
Email: cltktreviso@tin.it
www.padmanet.com
Director: Vania Tesser

Centro Muni Gyana
c/o Rosanna Giordano,
Viale Regina Margherita, 11/B,

90136 Palermo
Tel: (091) 336 883
Fax: (091) 637 5249
Email: centromunigyana@virgilio.it
www.padmanet.com/cmg
Director: Rosanna Giordano

Centro Studi Cenresig
Via A. Meucci 4
40138 Bologna
Tel: (051) 511 164
Email: luigichi@libero.it
www.padmanet.com/csc
Director: Luigi Chiarini

Centro Tara Cittamani
Via Mortise 34,
35100 Padova
Tel: (049) 850 805
Fax: (049) 880 4576
Email: taracit@libero.it
www.padmanet.com/ctc
Director: Filippo Scianna

Centro Terra di Unificazione Ewam
Via Cortine 8
50021 Barberina Val d'Elsa, Florence
Tel: (055) 807 5732
Fax: (0577) 933 831
Email: Longeva@tin.it
www.padmanet.com/ewam
Director: Marcello Macini
Resident teacher: Tulku Gyatso

Chiara Luce Edizioni
Via Poggiberna 9
56040 Pomaia (Pisa)
Tel/Fax: (050) 685 690
Email: chiara.luce@tiscalinet.it
www.chiaraluce.it
Director: Lorenzo Vasallo

Diamant Verlag
Bahnhofstraße 13a
39052 Kaltern,
Tel/Fax: (0471) 964 183
Email: c.well@iol.it
Director: Claudia Wellnitz

Istituto Lama Tzong Khapa
Via Poggiberna 9
56040 Pomaia (Pisa)
Tel: (050) 685 654
Fax: (050) 685 695
Res Tel: (050) 684 133
Email: iltk@libero.it

www.padmanet.com/iltk
Director: Maurizio Cacciatore
Resident teachers: Geshe Jampa Gyatso,
Geshe Tenzin Tenphel

A project of Istituto Lama Tzong Khapa:
Shenpen Samten Ling Nunnery
See above.
A project of Istituto Lama Tzong Khapa:
Takden Shedrup Targye Ling
See above.
Manager Ven. Olivier Rossi

Kushi Ling Retreat Centre
Alle Fontane
Laghel di sopra 19, 38062 Arco/Tn
Tel: (471) 964 183
Email: c.well@iol.it
Director: Claudia Wellnitz

Shiné
Via Poggiberna 9
56040 Pomaia (Pisa)
Tel: (050) 685 774
Fax: (050) 685 768
Email: shne@sirius.pisa.it
www.fpmt.org/shine
Director: Ven. Raffaello Longo

Universal Education Italy
Via Mortara n. 80
44100 Ferrara
Email: turchina@tin.it
Director: Stella Messina

Yeshe Norbu – Appello per il Tibet
Via Poggiberna 9
56040 Pomaia (Pisa)
Tel: (050) 685 033
Fax: (050) 685 768
Email: periltibet@libero.it
www.padmanet.com/yn
Director: Francesca Piatti

JAPAN 81
Do Ngak Sung Juk Centre
Nikkon Building, 9th Fl. #93
3-Chome 22-15 Shimoochiai
Shinjuku-ku, Tokyo
161-0033
Tel/Fax: (03) 5641 6707
Email: office@fpmt-japan.org
www.fpmt-japan.org
Director: Shoko Harding

LATVIA 371
Ganden Buddhist Meditation Centre

Brivibas iela 46 – 6
Riga, LV1011
Tel: 724 0415
Email: Ganden@dharmatours.com
www.dharmatours.com/Ganden
Director: Uldis Balodis

MALAYSIA 60
Losang Dragpa Centre
No.1, Lot 57, Jalan Hillside Estate, Taman
Melur, Ampang Jaya 68000,
Selangor
Tel/Fax: (03) 4257 3194
Email: ldc@pc.jaring.my
www.fpmt-mal.org
Director: Ven. Thubten Osel
Resident teacher: Samlo Geshe Kelsang

MEXICO 52
When calling from outside Mexico delete
"01"
Serlingpa Retreat Center
Alvaro Obregón 18-2
Col. Roma, Mexico City, C.P. 06700
Tel: (01) 7153 0581
Fax: (01) 5264 6764
Email: serlinpa@prodigy.net.mx
www.geocities.com/Heartland/Forest/
2253
Director: Rocio Arreola

Jangchub Ling Study Group
Articulo 123, no. 45 #27
Col. Centro
Mexico City 06050
Tel: (01) 5512 6939
Email: mayramexico@hotmail.com
Coordinator: Mayra Rocha

MONGOLIA 976
Please add "11" when dialing Mongolia
FPMT-Mongolia
Ganden Do Ngag Shedrup Ling
Post Box 219
Ulaan Bataar 13
Tel: 321 580
Fax: 314 115
Email: fpmt-mongolia@magicnet.mn
Director: Ueli Minder
Resident teacher: Geshe Nyima Dorje

NEPAL 977
Ganden Yiga Chözin Buddhist Meditation
Centre
Nr. Kharai Lakeside, Kaski District
Pokhara 6
Phone (mobile): 9810 25 146

Fax: (1) 410 992
Email: pokharacenter@yahoo.com
www.dharmatours/gyc
Manager: Ven Thubten Yeshe

Himalayan Buddhist Meditation Centre
Kamaladi Ganesthan
PO Box 817, Kathmandu
Tel: (1) 221 875
Fax: (1) 251 409
Email: hbmc@mos.com.np
www.dharmatours.com/hbmc
Director: Pooja Manandhar

Khachoe Ghakyil Nunnery
GPO Box 817, Kathmandu
Tel: (1) 481 236
Fax: (1) 481 267
www.members.tripod.com/~Lhamo/
Nuns/index.htm
Manager: Ven. Jangsem

Kopan Monastery
GPO Box 817, Kathmandu
Tel: (1) 481 268
Fax: (1) 481 267
Email: kopan@ecomail.com.np
www.kopan-monastery.com
Abbot/ resident teacher: Geshe Lhundrup
Rigsel

Lawudo Retreat Centre
GPO Box 817, Kathmandu
Tel: (1) 221 875
Fax: (1) 251 409
Director: Lama Kyabje Zopa Rinpoche

Thubten Shedrup Ling Monastery
Tibetan Camp
PO Box 2, Chaisala, Salleri
Solu Khumbu
Email: friends@shedrupling-monastery.org
www.shedrupling-monastery.org
Abbot: Geshe Lobsang Jamyang

NETHERLANDS 31
Maitreya Instituut Amsterdam
Brouwergracht 157-159
1015 GG Amsterdam
Tel: (020) 428 0842
Fax: (020) 428 2788
Email: amsterdam@maitreya.nl
www.maitreya.nl/adam
Director: Paula de Wys-Koolkin

Maitreya Instituut Emst
Heemhoeveweg 2, 8166 HA Emst

Tel: (0578) 661 450
Fax: (0578) 661 851
Email: emst@maitreya.nl
www.maitreya.nl
Director: Herman Homan
Resident teacher: Geshe Sonam Gyaltsen

NEW ZEALAND 64
Amitabha Hospice Service
6 Lyttleton Ave., Forrest Hill,
Auckland 1309
Tel: (09) 410 1431
Fax: (09) 410 1432
Email: amitabha@stupa.org.nz
www.amitabhahospice.org
Director: Ecie Hursthouse

Chandrakirti Tibetan Buddhist Meditation
Centre
PO Box 3319, Richmond, Nelson
Tel: (03) 543 2015
Fax: (03) 543 2016
Email: Chandrakirti@Tasman.net
Directors: Phillipa Rutherford & Bruce Farley

Dorje Chang Institute
56 Powell Street, Avondale (Auckland)
Tel/Fax: (09) 828 3333
Email: dci@dci.org.nz
www.dci.org.nz
Director: Kathy Frewen
Resident teacher: Geshe Thubten
Wangchen

Mahamudra Centre
Colville RD 4, Coromandel
Tel/Fax: (07) 866 6851
Email: retreat@mahamudra.org.nz
www.mahamudra.org.nz
Director: Terry Leach

RUSSIA 7
Ganden Tendar Ling Study Group
Lomonosovskii prospect, 19-39,
Moscow 117311
Tel: (095) 930-18-11
Email: gandentendarling@rambler.ru
Coordinator: Tatyana Petrova

SINGAPORE 65
Amitabha Buddhist Centre
494-D Geylang Road
Singapore 389 452
Tel: 745 8547
Fax: 741 0438
Email: fpmtsing@singnet.com.sg
www.fpmtabc.sg

Director: Hup Cheng Tan
Resident teacher: Geshe Thubten Chonyi

SPAIN 34
Centro Vajrayoguini
C/ Laforja, 118 bajos
08021 Barcelona
Tel: (93) 201 2005
Email: vajrayoguini@autocuracion.com
www.geocities.com/vajrayoguini
Director: Mercedes Udaeta

Ediciones Dharma
Elias Abad, 3 bajos
03660 Novelda (Alicante)
Tel: (96) 560 3200
Email: xavi@edicionesdharma.com
www.edicionesdharma.com
Director: Xavi Alongina

Khorlo Dompa Centro de Retiros
Calle Francisco Caravace no. 29
30600 Archena (Murcia)
Tel: (96) 860 8458
Email: khorlodompa@hotmail.com
Director: Maria Nieto Jara

Nagarjuna C.E.T. Alicante
C/Tte. Alvarez Soto 5 2o Izq.
Alicante
Email: nuan@retemail.es
Director: Ven. Angeles de la Torre

Nagarjuna C.E.T. Barcelona
Rosselon 298, Pral.2a
08037 Barcelona
Tel/Fax: (93) 457 0788
Email: cet-nagar-barna@ctv.es
www.ctv.es/USERS/cet-nagar-barna
Director: Rosalia Posa
Resident teacher: Geshe Lobsang Tsultrim

Nagarjuna C.E.T. Granada
Manuel de Falla 12 4o Dcha Apartado de
Correos 1112
18080 Granada
Tel: (95) 825 1629
Fax: (95) 841 1179
Email: nagargra@arrakis.es
Director: Ven. Gloria Mallol

Nagarjuna C.E.T. Madrid
C/Duque de Osuna 8, Ext., 2o Izq.
28015 Madrid
Tel/Fax: (91) 541 3755
Email: nagarma@batch-pc.es
www.sapiens.ya.com/nagarjuna

Director: Ven. Thubten Palden
Resident teacher: Geshe Tsering Palden
Nagarjuna C.E.T. Valencia
C/ General Urrutia, 43 ptas 1 y 2
46006 Valencia
Tel/Fax: (96) 395 1008
Email: nagarval@airtel.net
www.geocities.com/nagaryuna
Director: Alfredo Medrano
Resident teacher: Geshe Lamsang

O.Sel.Ling Centro de Retiros
Apartado 99
18400 Orgiva (Granada)
Tel/Fax: (95) 834 3134
Email: oseling@teleline.es
Director: Ven. Paloma Alba
Resident teacher: Geshe Tega

Tekchen Chö Ling Study Group
Calle Tomas Valls 12, 4-7
46870 Ontinyent (Valencia)
Tel: (96) 291 3231
Coordinators: Juan & Paloma Bas

Thubten Shen Phen Ling Study Group
Paseo Marques de Corvera, 50-3o
30002 Murcia
Tel: (96) 834 4696
Fax: (96) 829 4515
Email: thubtenshen@inicia.es
Coordinator: Emilia Cotorruelo

Tushita Retreat Center
Mas Casa nova d'en Crous
Ap. Correos, 69
17401 Arbúcies (Girona)
Tel: (97) 217 8262
Fax: (93) 889 5203
Email: tushitaes@interausa.com
Director: Kiko Segura

SWEDEN (46)
Tsog Nyi Ling Study Group
Osterby 103
S 73398 Ransta (Vasteras)
Tel: 0224 200 22
Email: tsognyiling@swipnet.se
Coordinator: Gun Cissé

SWITZERLAND (41)
Longku Study Group
Zentrum fur Buddhismus
Reiterstr. 2
Bern 3013
Tel: 31 931 04 75
Email: ruhofer@bluewin.ch

http://www.zentrumfuerbuddhismus.ch/f
pmt
Coordinator: Ruth Hofer

TAIWAN 886
Hayagriva Study Group
8F, No.720 Chong-Cheng Road
Taoyuan City
Tel: (03) 316 5506
Email: fpmtty@ms65.hinet.net
Coordinator: Shen, Mei-Chen

Heruka Center
No. 70, Ying-Der Street,
Kaohsiung 806
Tel: (07) 713 4861
Fax: (07) 713 4917
Email: fpmtks@ms65.hinet.net
Director and resident teacher: Geshe
Lobsang Jamyang

Jinsiu Farlin
F12-1, (space) No 81, Section 3
Pa-Te Road, Taipei 105
Tel: (02) 2577 0333
Fax: (02) 2577 0510
Email: jinsiufa@ms3.hinet.net
http://home.kimo.com.tw/fpmttaiwan
Director: Mike Wang
Abbot: Lama Zopa Rinpoche
Resident teacher: Geshe Thubten Gyurme

Shakyamuni Center
No.29 Wen-Hsin South 3 Road,
Taichung 408
Tel: (04) 2471 8050
Fax: (04) 2471 8051
Email: fpmttc@ms65.hinet.net
Director: Ven. Thubten Kachoe
Resident teacher: Geshe Dadak

Universal Education-Alice Project
No. 27, Huan-Shan Road, Neihu District,
Taipei 114
Tel: (02) 2799 1817 x 601
Email: chhk915@mail.apol.com.tw
Director: Hei-Kai Cheng

UNITED STATES 1
Buddha Maitreya Study Group
PO Box 2892, Amherst,
MA 01004-2892
Tel: (413) 586 4596
Email Jhamdol@aol.com
Coordinator: Jhamba Dolkar

Dharma Vision
246 C Ledoux Street
Taos, NM 87571
Tel: (505) 737 0550
Email: ChristinaL@fpmt.org
Director: Christina Lundberg

Enlightened Experience Celebration 4
c/o FPMT International Office
P.O. Box 888,
Taos, NM, 87571
Email: fpmtinfo@fpmt.org

Guhyasamaya Center
6741 Stone Maple Terrace
Centreville, VA 20121
Tel: (703) 815 0758
Voice Mail: (703) 502 4900
Email: maniwheel@aol.com
Director: Lorne Ladner

Gyalwa Gyatso Buddhist Center
PO Box 41307
San Jose, CA 95160
Tel: (408) 792 3460
Fax: (209) 844 3988
Email: ggbc@lamrim.com
www.gyalwagyatso.org
Director: Linda Hoeber

Kadampa Center
7404-G Chapel Hill Road
Raleigh, NC 27607
Tel: (919) 859 3433
Fax: (919) 460 1769
Email: 73571.701@compuserve.com
www.kadampa-center.org
Director: Robbie Watkins
Resident teacher: Geshe Gelek Chodak

Ksitigarbha Study Group
Box 6608
Taos, NM 87571
Tel: (505) 751 0403
Email: merc@laplaza.org
Coordinators: Anthony Mercolino and
Toby Downes

Kurukulla Center
68 Magoun Ave, Medford,
MA 02155
Tel: (617) 624 0177
Fax: (617) 776 7841
Email: kkc@kurukulla.org
www.kurukulla.org
Director: Wendy Cook
Resident teacher: Geshe Tsulga

Lama Yeshe Wisdom Archive
PO Box 356
Weston, MA 02493
Tel: (781) 899 9587
Email: info@LamaYeshe.com
www.LamaYeshe.com
Director: Nicholas Ribush

Land of Calm Abiding
PO Box 123
San Simeon, CA 93452
Director: John Jackson

Land of Medicine Buddha
5800 Prescott Road
Soquel, CA 95073
Tel: (831) 462 8383
Fax: (831) 462 8380
Email: LMB@medicinebuddha.org
www.medicinebuddha.org
Director: Sally Barraud

Liberation Prison Project
PO Box 31527
San Francisco, CA 94131
Phone: (415) 337 1725
Email: Liberationpp@compuserve.com
Director: Ven. Robina Courtin

Milarepa Center
Barnet Mountain

Barnet, VT 05821
Tel: (802) 633 4136
Fax: (802) 633 3808
Email: Milarepa@kingcon.com
www.milarepacenter.org
Director: John Feuille

Osel Shen Phen Ling
PO Box 5776, Missoula, MT 59806
Tel: (406) 327 1204
Email: osel@fpmt-osel.org
www.fpmt-osel.org
Director: Deanna Sheriff

Tara Redwood School
5800 Prescott Road
Soquel, CA 95073
Tel/Fax: (831) 462 9632
Email: taraschool@cs.com

The Karuna Group
1840 41st. Ave., 102-267
Capitola, CA 95010
Tel: (831) 457 7750
Email: karuna@thekarunagroup.com
Director: Karuna Cayton

Thubten Norbu Ling Tibetan Buddhist Center
430 Alta Vista,
Santa Fe, NM 87501

Tel: (505) 570 6000
Email: tnlsf@yahoo.com
www.tnlsf.org
Director: Steven Johnson
Resident teacher: Geshe Thubten Sherab

Tilopa Study Group
201 North Morgan,
Virginia, Il 62691
Tel: (217) 414 3853
Email: chonyicpa@hotmail.com
Coordinater: Ven. Thubten Kunga

Tsa Tsa Studio/Center for Tibetan Sacred Art
4 Joost Ave, San Francisco, CA 94131
Tel: (877) 662 4486
Email: tsatsafpmt@aol.com
www.tsatsastudio.org
Director: Roberta Raine

Tse Chen Ling
4 Joost Ave, San Francisco, CA 94131
Tel: (415) 333 3261
Fax: (415) 333 4851
Email: tclcenter@aol.com
www.tsechenling.com
Director: Ven. Lobsang Chokyi
Resident teacher: Geshe Ngawang Dakpa

Tubten Kunga Center
835 SE 8th Avenue
Deerfield Beach, FL 33441
Tel: (954) 421 6224
Fax: (954) 421 7718
Email: tubtenkunga@aol.com
www.tubtenkunga.org
Director: Maggie Alarcon
Resident teacher: Geshe Konchog Kyab

Vajrapani Institute
PO Box 2130
Boulder Creek, CA 95006
Tel: (831) 338 6654
Fax: (831) 338 3666
Email: vajrapani@vajrapani.org
www.vajrapani.org
Director: Ven. Amy Miller

Wisdom Publications Inc
199 Elm Street
Somerville, MA 02144
Tel: (617) 776 7416
Sales USA Tel: (800) 272 4050
Fax: (617) 776 7841
Email: info@wisdompubs.org
www.wisdompubs.org
Director: Tim McNeill

Maitreya Project Offices

Maitreya Project
Bodhgaya, Gaya District
Bihar, 824 231
Tel: (91)(631) 200 727/620/621
Fax: (91) (631) 200 774
Email: maitreya@vsnl.com
Contact: Ven. Marcel Bertels

Maitreya Project International
PO Box 98690, TST, Hong Kong
Email: pkedge@compuserve.com
www.maitreyaproject.org
Director: Peter Kedge

Maitreya Project Taiwan Office
1F, No.3, Alley14, Lane 75, Sec4,
Nan-Jing East Road, Taipei 105
Tel: (02) 8770 6939
Fax: (02) 2546 9223
Email: mpbuddha@tpts6.seed.net.tw
Director: Klaus Liu

FPMT Libraries

India
Tushita Meditation Centre,
Dharamsala
(Contact details under India)

Nepal
A.G. Lodge
Namche Bazaar

Thame Lodge
Lukla c/o Himalayan Buddhist
Meditation Centre, PO Box 4597
Kathmandu, Nepal

Tel: (977) (1) 221 875
Fax: (977) (1) 410 992

Index

Italicised page references refer to illustrations and * asterisked terms to the glossary.